First World War
and Army of Occupation
War Diary
France, Belgium and Germany

28 DIVISION
83 Infantry Brigade
King's Own (Royal Lancaster Regiment)
1/5th Battalion
14 February 1915 - 31 October 1915

WO95/2274/3

The Naval & Military Press Ltd
www.nmarchive.com
Published in association with The National Archives

Published by

The Naval & Military Press Ltd

Unit 10 Ridgewood Industrial Park,

Uckfield, East Sussex,

TN22 5QE England

Tel: +44 (0) 1825 749494

www.naval-military-press.com

www.nmarchive.com

This diary has been reprinted in facsimile from the original. Any imperfections are inevitably reproduced and the quality may fall short of modern type and cartographic standards.

© Crown Copyright
Images reproduced by permission of The National Archives, London, England, 2015.

Contents

Document type	Place/Title	Date From	Date To
Heading	WO95/2274/3		
Heading	28th Division 83rd Infy Bde 1/5th Bn King's Own R. L. R. Feb-Oct 1915 To 55 Division 166 Bde Box 2930		
Heading	83rd Bde. 28th Div. War Diary Joined 83rd Inf. Bde. /3/15 1/5th K. O. R. L. 14th To 28th February 1915 Oct 15		
War Diary	Sevenoaks	14/02/1915	14/02/1915
War Diary	Havre	15/02/1915	16/02/1915
War Diary	Havre To Winnezeele	17/02/1915	17/02/1915
War Diary	Winnezeele	18/02/1915	28/02/1915
Heading	83rd Bde. 28th Div. War Diary Bde. Temporarily Attached To 5th Division 1/5th K. O. R. L. March 1915		
War Diary	Winnezeele	01/03/1915	02/03/1915
War Diary	Bailleul	03/03/1915	07/03/1915
War Diary	St Jans Cappel	08/03/1915	10/03/1915
War Diary	Dranoutre	11/03/1915	14/03/1915
War Diary	St Jans Cappel	15/03/1915	17/03/1915
War Diary	Dranoutre	18/03/1915	20/03/1915
War Diary	Neuve Eglise	21/03/1915	22/03/1915
War Diary	Ravelsberg	23/03/1915	31/03/1915
Heading	28th Division 5th Royal Lancs. Vol III 1-30.4.15		
War Diary	Ravetsbergh	01/04/1915	02/04/1915
War Diary	Boeschepe	03/04/1915	09/04/1915
War Diary	Ypres	10/04/1915	20/04/1915
War Diary	St. Jean	21/04/1915	22/04/1915
War Diary	C 21 C. N Of St. Jean	23/04/1915	26/04/1915
War Diary	Potize	27/04/1915	28/04/1915
War Diary	Huts In H. 5.	29/04/1915	30/04/1915
Heading	1/5th Royal Lancs Vol IV 1-31.5.15		
War Diary	Huts H5	01/05/1915	01/05/1915
War Diary	Huts H5 Frezenberg	02/05/1915	02/05/1915
War Diary	Frezenberg	03/05/1915	05/05/1915
War Diary	Huts In H5	06/05/1915	06/05/1915
War Diary	Huts In H5 St Jean	07/05/1915	07/05/1915
War Diary	St Jean	08/05/1915	08/05/1915
War Diary	Huts In H5	09/05/1915	10/05/1915
War Diary	Potijze	11/05/1915	11/05/1915
War Diary	Huts at G5	12/05/1915	12/05/1915
War Diary	Near Poperinghe	13/05/1915	13/05/1915
War Diary	Ryveld	14/05/1915	20/05/1915
War Diary	Ryveld Vlamertinghe	21/05/1915	21/05/1915
War Diary	Vlamertinghe	22/05/1915	23/05/1915
War Diary	I 24	23/05/1915	25/05/1915
War Diary	G.H.Q. Line	26/05/1915	31/05/1915
Heading	83rd Bde. 28th Div. War Diary 1/5th K.O.R.L. June 1915		
War Diary	Zillebeke	01/06/1915	01/06/1915
War Diary	Zillebeke Ouderdom H 19	02/06/1915	02/06/1915
War Diary	Ouderdom Ryveld	03/06/1915	03/06/1915
War Diary	Ryveld	04/06/1915	13/06/1915

War Diary	Ryveld Huts M.6.a.	14/06/1915	14/06/1915
War Diary	Huts M.6.a.	15/06/1915	19/06/1915
War Diary	Huts M. 6. a. Locre	20/06/1915	20/06/1915
War Diary	Locre	21/06/1915	23/06/1915
War Diary	Locre La Clytte	24/06/1915	24/06/1915
War Diary	La Clytte	25/06/1915	30/06/1915
Heading	83rd Bde. 28th Div. War Diary 5th K. O. R. L. July 1915		
War Diary	La Clytte	01/07/1915	20/07/1915
War Diary	La Clytte Kemmel	21/07/1915	21/07/1915
War Diary	Kemmel	22/07/1915	30/07/1915
War Diary	Scherpenberg Bivouacs	31/07/1915	31/07/1915
Operation(al) Order(s)	Operation Order No. 1 By Major General Commdg 5th Kings Own	21/07/1915	21/07/1915
Heading	83rd Bde. 28th Div. War Diary 1/5th K. O. R. L. August 1915		
Heading	War Diary August 1915 5th Bn. The King's Own Rl. Lancs. Regt.		
War Diary	Scherpenberg Bivouacs	01/08/1915	03/08/1915
War Diary	Scherpenberg Locre	04/08/1915	04/08/1915
War Diary	Locre	05/08/1915	10/08/1915
War Diary	Locre Scherpenberg	11/08/1915	11/08/1915
War Diary	Scherpenberg	12/08/1915	17/08/1915
War Diary	Kemmel (Right Sector)	17/08/1915	22/08/1915
War Diary	Scherpenberg	23/08/1915	28/08/1915
War Diary	Kemmel (Right Sector)	29/08/1915	31/08/1915
Operation(al) Order(s)	Operation Orders No. 2 By Major C.C. Cadman Comdg 5th King's Own (RLR)	03/08/1915	03/08/1915
Operation(al) Order(s)	Operation Orders No. 3 By Major Cadman Comdg. 5th Bn The Kings Own (R L R)	10/08/1915	10/08/1915
Operation(al) Order(s)	Operation Orders No. 4 By Major E.C. Cadman Cmdg. 5th Bn. The Kings Own (R L R)	15/08/1915	15/08/1915
Operation(al) Order(s)	Operation Orders No. 5 By Major E.C. Cadman Cmdg. 5th Bn. The Kings Own (R L R)	17/08/1915	17/08/1915
Operation(al) Order(s)	Operation Order No. 6 By Major E.C. Cadman Commanding 1/5th Bn The Kings Own R. Lancs Regt.		
Operation(al) Order(s)	Operation Orders No. 7 By Major E.C Cadman Cmdg 5th Bn The Kings Own (R L R)	28/08/1915	28/08/1915
Operation(al) Order(s)	Operation Orders No. 13 By M. Col. Cadman Cmdg. 5th Kings Own (RLR)		
Heading	83rd Bde. 28th Div. War Diary 1/5th K. O. R. L. September 1915		
War Diary	Kemmel	01/09/1915	03/09/1915
War Diary	Scherpenberg	04/09/1915	23/09/1915
War Diary	Outtersteene	24/09/1915	26/09/1915
War Diary	Robecq	27/09/1915	30/09/1915
Heading	83rd Bde. 28th Div. War Diary Battalion Transferred To 2nd Bde. 1st Div. 21.10.15 1/5th K. O. R. L. October 1915		
War Diary	Vermelles	01/10/1915	01/10/1915
War Diary	Annequin	02/10/1915	02/10/1915
War Diary	Vermelles (Hulluch Trenches)	03/10/1915	03/10/1915
War Diary	Hulluch Trenches	04/10/1915	05/10/1915
War Diary	Annequin	06/10/1915	06/10/1915
War Diary	Gonnehem (Cense Le Vallee)	07/10/1915	14/10/1915
War Diary	Gonnehem Cense Le Vallee Ferme du Roi	15/10/1915	15/10/1915

War Diary	Ferme du Roi (Bethune)	16/10/1915	16/10/1915
War Diary	Ferme Du Roi	17/10/1915	17/10/1915
War Diary	Le Preol	17/10/1915	20/10/1915
War Diary	Gonnehem L'Ecleme-Robecq	21/10/1915	21/10/1915
War Diary	L'Ecleme-Robecq	21/10/1915	21/10/1915
War Diary	L'Ecleme-Robecq Ecquedecques	22/10/1915	22/10/1915
War Diary	Ecquedecques	23/10/1915	31/10/1915
Operation(al) Order(s)	Operation Order No. 78 By Brigadier General H.S.L. Ravenshaw. C.M.G. Commanding 83rd Infantry Brigade	15/10/1915	15/10/1915
Operation(al) Order(s)	Operation Orders No. 79 By Brigadier General H.S.L. Ravenshaw, C.M.G. Commanding 83rd Infantry Brigade	16/10/1915	16/10/1915
Operation(al) Order(s)	83rd Brigade Operation Order No. 80	20/10/1915	20/10/1915
Miscellaneous			
Miscellaneous	Machine Guns Will Be Relieved As Follows		
Operation(al) Order(s)	After Operation Order No. 80 83rd Brigade	20/10/1915	20/10/1915

W095/22741/3

28TH DIVISION
83RD INFY BDE

Royal Lancaster Regt

1/5TH BN KING'S OWN R.L.R.
FEB - OCT 1915

To 55 DIVISION
166 BDE

Box 2930

83rd Bde.
28th Div.

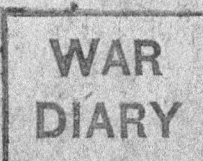

WAR DIARY

Joined 83rd Inf. Bde. /3/15.

1/5th K. O. R. L.

14th to 28th F E B R U A R Y

1 9 1 5

Army Form C. 2118.

WAR DIARY
or
INTELLIGENCE SUMMARY

(Erase heading not required.)

Instructions regarding War Diaries and Intelligence Summaries are contained in F. S. Regs., Part II. and the Staff Manual respectively. Title pages will be prepared in manuscript.

Hour, Date, Place	Summary of Events and Information	Remarks and references to Appendices
Sunday 14.2.1915 SEVENOAKS	Battalion entrained for SOUTHAMPTON. — 3 trains. Last train left SEVENOAKS 9.42 A.M. arrived SOUTHAMPTON 2.50 p.m. Sailed from Southampton for HAVRE 7.45 p.m.	Strength of Battalion. Officers 29 N C O's & men 1037 = 1066
Monday 15.2.1915 HAVRE	Arrived HAVRE 10 a.m. — Received orders 11 A.M. proceeded to No 1 Camp 2.30 p.m.	Horses Riding 14 Draught Pack 16 6 G.S. Wagons 11 Limbered Wagons 2 M. Guns 2 Musical Carts 1 Water Carts 2 Mess Carts (Officers) 2
Tuesday 16.2.1915 HAVRE	Battalion parade 7.30 A.M. Roll call. Rest of day spent in completing distribution of necessaries. Orders received at 1 A.M. to entrain to move off at 1 A.M. to entrain at 3 A.M. (less 2 Platoons). The two Platoons will follow at 4 p.m. 17th inst	
Wednesday 17.2.1915 HAVRE & WINNEZEELE	2.15 A.M. arrived HAVRE station Point No 1. Entrained & moved off 7.15 A.M. Vans to carry 36 N.C.O men. Reached BAYINGHOVE Station 7 A.M 18.2.15.	
Thursday 18.2.15 WINNEZEELE	10.30 A.M. The Battalion marched to WINNEZEELE arriving Billets in Barns.	

Army Form C. 2118.

WAR DIARY
or
INTELLIGENCE SUMMARY

(Erase heading not required.)

Instructions regarding War Diaries and Intelligence Summaries are contained in F. S. Regs., Part II. and the Staff Manual respectively. Title pages will be prepared in manuscript.

Hour, Date, Place	Summary of Events and Information	Remarks and references to Appendices
WEDNESDAY 24.2.15	9 A.M. – 12.30 Noon. – Route march 9 miles. Rest of day spent in cleaning equipment. Heavy snow storm throughout the march.	
THURSDAY 25.2.15	The early part of the day was spent in cleaning billets, washing clothing &c. Night entrenching.	
FRIDAY 26.2.15	10 A.M. – 5 P.M. Route march & entrenching.	
SATURDAY 27.2.15	10 A.M. Route march 5 miles. 12 A.M. Orders received to be ready to move on to BAILLEUL. 3.45 P.M. The above orders cancelled.	
SUNDAY 28.2.15	R.C. Church Parade 9.45 A.M.	

Army Form C. 2118.

WAR DIARY
or
INTELLIGENCE SUMMARY

(Erase heading not required.)

Instructions regarding War Diaries and Intelligence Summaries are contained in F. S. Regs., Part II. and the Staff Manual respectively. Title pages will be prepared in manuscript.

Hour, Date, Place	Summary of Events and Information	Remarks and references to Appendices
WINNEZEELE THURSDAY 18.2.15	Sent two Platoons nearer WINNEZEELE at 8 p.m.	
FRIDAY 19.2.15	9 a.m. Kit inspection & Rifle inspection. Completing service arrangements - 2 p.m. Route march 7 miles.	
SATURDAY 20.2.15	Morning: Inspection of billets by C.O. Afternoon. 2 p.m. to 6 p.m. Route march 6 miles with two hours entrenching.	
SUNDAY 21.2.15	8.45 a.m. Route march 6 miles. Entrenching 5 hours. Returned to billets 5 p.m.	
MONDAY 22.2.15	9.15 a.m. to 4.45 p.m. Battalion route march. Ordered formation re: shrapnel by General — lunch - Dominion.	
TUESDAY 23.2.15	9 a.m. Route march 6 miles. Entrenching 3 hours. Returned to billets 7 p.m.	

1247 W 3299 200,000 (E) 8/14 J.P.C. & A. Forms/C. 2118/11.

Army Form C. 2118.

WAR DIARY
or
INTELLIGENCE SUMMARY

(Erase heading not required.)

Instructions regarding War Diaries and Intelligence Summaries are contained in F. S. Regs., Part II. and the Staff Manual respectively. Title pages will be prepared in manuscript.

Hour, Date, Place	Summary of Events and Information	Remarks and references to Appendices
SUNDAY 26.2.15	11.30 a.m. a blue occupied by two platoons of D Coy was heavily shelled — name of trench owner DECONVELAIN AIME. (one of enquiry from for Mummy (1.3.15). 4 p.m - 9.30 p.m Rents moved & men occupying & widening Trenches	

Michael Howard D Colonel Commanding 5/ The Kings own Regt.

83rd Bde.
28th Div.

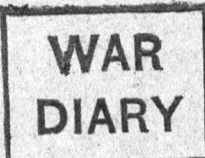

Bde. temporarily attached to 5th Division.

1/5th K.O.R.L.

MARCH

1915

Army Form C. 2118.

WAR DIARY
or
INTELLIGENCE SUMMARY

(Erase heading not required.)

Instructions regarding War Diaries and Intelligence Summaries are contained in F. S. Regs., Part II. and the Staff Manual respectively. Title pages will be prepared in manuscript.

Hour, Date, Place	Summary of Events and Information	Remarks and references to Appendices
Nimègues March 1-15 9.30 am	Course of enquiry re Pte R. C. Miller	
9.30 am to 1 pm	A.P.M. Makes enquiries	
	He is of opinion that Reynolds case can establish there was no foul play. Men occupied. Toilet	
March 2	Left Nimègues 10 am arrived Bailleul 11.15 am [The troops were billeted in Police building. 3 O. in the School & 1 Coy in
4.10 am	Kinane Asylum]	
Bailleul March 3		
7.30 am	Roll Call	
8.30 am	Left Inspection. CO attended funeral & place to take instruction	
	from Col. 15th Infantry Brigade	
March 4		
7.30 am	Roll Call	
10 am to 10.30 pm	Route March. CO. Adjutant & officers then NCOs attend for French instruction during night	
March 5		
7.30 am	Roll Call	
10 am	Route march - Producers artillery formation. Officers &
10½ pm	10 NCOs for French instruction	
March 6		
	Lecture @ rec. Battalion officers club - set on trench work	
2.45 pm	& developed trench instruction at Nimègues	
11 pm	Return of officer & NCOs from french instruction	

1247 W 3299 200,000 (E) 8/14 J.B.C. & A. Forms/C. 2118/1.

WAR DIARY
or
INTELLIGENCE SUMMARY

(Erase heading not required.)

Army Form C. 2118.

Hour, Date, Place	Summary of Events and Information	Remarks and references to Appendices
Radinghem March 7-13	"A" Coy Wulverghem Billets. Trenches 6 to 10 for which work 1-4/1. "C" Coy Wulverghem for trench work. Remainder 3" Coy in trenches. Walked St Jan Cappel.	
St Jan Cappel March 8 1.30 pm	"A" Coy proceeded to St Cappel for trench work 9 hrs drawn.	1200 wounded
March 9	"A" Coy returns approx at its quarters. Toppers Neto. "C" Coy do.	one killed
March 10	Wounded in head & left paralysis. "A" Coy reports inspection. Cleaner & equipment. "C" Coy returned after trench inspection. "A" Coy left billets at Jan Cappel for Dramoutre.	
Dramoutre March 11 3.30 pm	"A" Coy arrived from Wulverghem marched by Jansu then "S" Coy left for trench work. A young Subaltern.	two killed
March 12	"C" Coy at trenches (note of reflex respiration moving increase in physical dull)	
March 13	"A" Coy in minor duty relieved. "A" Coy returned.	
March 14	Received orders billets for St Jan Cappel at 2.00 pm.	
St Jan Cappel March 15	A Coy march to St Jan Cappel, A & D march duty.	two killed
March 16	B & D trenches. A & B relief.	one wounded
March 17	B Coy left trenches for billets, "A" Coy on active albuminuria. "C" & A left for trenches to relieve A & B Coy. A post line. Our support.	3 wounded

Army Form C. 2118.

WAR DIARY
or
INTELLIGENCE SUMMARY

(Erase heading not required.)

Instructions regarding War Diaries and Intelligence Summaries are contained in F. S. Regs., Part II. and the Staff Manual respectively. Title pages will be prepared in manuscript.

Hour, Date, Place	Summary of Events and Information	Remarks and references to Appendices
Grancourt March 18	A. C. Coy. together B Coy in support from hillock in front B & exchanges trenches out 10	one wounded
March 19	went into support	
March 20	A Coy in trenches N.E. in nature is Coy in Killen	2 wounded
Hame Place March 21	B Coy relieved 1/3 of 10a. B Coy up from 8 & 9. A relieve Border	
March 22	5	
	The Battalion carried march with us same orders as previous day. Relieved by 2.5 Northumberlands at 9.15pm proceeded to Hinacourt arrived at 7am 23rd inst. Battalion report no further	12 wounded
Hinacourt March 23	D	
24		
25	4 pm scouting (A B C) fire opened Turks with M.G from Herre	
26	7.28 Returned 1.30am distance 12 miles	3/4
	Battalion march no killed	
27	Battalion left next relief for trenches roop of Watergallin March 29	
	3.30pm arrived at 8 pm Trefina. A Coy & 9 Rifleman Kla. No 10a	
	B Coy in support Seventh farm C Coy hand stations Jam with one platoon each one wounded since died	
28	Dispositions similar to previous day. A Coy on fatigue C Coy at platoon	
	One Platoon 9 support. 2nd platoon duty with Rt. C Coy communication trench	
29	A.10 Coy in trenches B Coy fatigue one platoon 10A C Coy 3 platoons	
	with R.E. communication trenches. One platoon fatigue from 7 10A	One killed 3 wounded
30	Dispositions same as yesterday.	no wounded
31		

Reviewed by a Thorworth Regt.

Richard J Freuden L. Col.
Royal Lancashire Regiment

12/5/08

1st (Mainland)
2nd Division.

5th Royal Lancs.

Vol III 1 — 30.4.15

Army Form C. 2118.

WAR DIARY
or
INTELLIGENCE SUMMARY

(Erase heading not required.)

Instructions regarding War Diaries and Intelligence Summaries are contained in F. S. Regs., Part II. and the Staff Manual respectively. Title pages will be prepared in manuscript.

Hour, Date, Place		Summary of Events and Information	Remarks and references to Appendices
1-4-15.	RAVETSBERGH.	Resting.	
2-4-15.	RAVETSBERGH.	Resting. Church Parade (Voluntary) 10 A.M. Battalion left RAVETSBERGH at 3 p.m. for billets at BOESCHEPE. Arrived 6 p.m.	
3-4-15.	BOESCHEPE.	Resting.	
4-4-15.	BOESCHEPE.	Resting. Church Parade. Communion 8-15 a.m., Service 10-45 a.m.	
5-4-15.	BOESCHEPE.	Resting.	
6-4-15.	BOESCHEPE.	Resting. Bathing Parade. Company Drill & musketry under O. C. Coys.	
7-4-15.	BOESCHEPE.	Resting. Inspection of Brigade by General Smith-Dorrien followed by address to Officers and a number of N.C.O's	
8-4-15.	BOESCHEPE.	Resting. Bayonet exercise and Company Drill. Short route marches.	
9-4-15.	BOESCHEPE.	Left BOESCHEPE for YPRES 8-30 a.m. Arrived 12-30 Noon. Billeted in schools. Remainder of day spent in cleaning up billets, which were very dirty.	

Army Form C. 2118.

WAR DIARY
or
INTELLIGENCE SUMMARY

(Erase heading not required.)

Instructions regarding War Diaries and Intelligence Summaries are contained in F. S. Regs., Part II. and the Staff Manual respectively. Title pages will be prepared in manuscript.

Hour, Date, Place	Summary of Events and Information	Remarks and references to Appendices
10-4-15. YPRES.	Billets. Company drill – handling of arms, and lectures. Ten (10) Officers for trench Instruction at 5 p.m.	
11-4-15. YPRES.	One Company for fatigue. Resting. One Company on fatigue. No Sunday service! Why ? .	
12-4-15. YPRES.	Battalion moved for trench duties 8-30 p.m., by Companies at 4 hour intervals. Completed relief of Monmouth Regt at 2-45 a.m. This delay was caused by the Mons. guide being inexperienced. Trenches :- B Coy. on the Right. C " " Left A " in Support. D " in Reserve. Casualties :- Wounded, two men. These men were wounded in going up to the trenches.	
13-4-15. YPRES.	Trench duties. Disposition as on 12th inst. C. Coy trenches were heavily shelled by trench mortars Casualties :- 2 Killed – (died of wounds.) 15 Wounded.	

Army Form C. 2118.

WAR DIARY
or
INTELLIGENCE SUMMARY
(Erase heading not required.)

Instructions regarding War Diaries and Intelligence Summaries are contained in F. S. Regs., Part II. and the Staff Manual respectively. Title pages will be prepared in manuscript.

Hour, Date, Place	Summary of Events and Information	Remarks and references to Appendices
13-4-15. YPRES. (continued)	Heavy shelling throughout the day. Great shortage of sandbags. Parapets unhealthy. Require strengthening.	
14-4-15. YPRES.	Trenches at YPRES. Disposition as on 12th inst. Casualties. 4 killed & 1 died of wounds. 18 wounded. A coy. working party on dug-outs in wrood, were fired on by German Infantry - shrapnel. Nine rounds rapid fire about 3 p.m.	
15-4-15. YPRES.	Dispositions:- B & C coys. in trenches, A coy. were taken from the supports and strengthened "C" coy line. "D" coy. were moved up from the Reserve position to support - occupying communication trench immediately behind the left of our line. Casualties:- Wounded:- 5 men.	
16-4-15. YPRES.	Dispositions:- "B" and "C" coys. in firing line. "B" coy. were relieved by "A" coy. during the night, and "C" coy by "D" coy. "B" coy in support. "C" coy. 3 Platoons in Support. 1 Platoon in Reserve. Casualties:- 1 killed & 3 died of wounds. 14 wounded.	

Army Form C. 2118.

WAR DIARY
or
INTELLIGENCE SUMMARY

(Erase heading not required.)

Instructions regarding War Diaries and Intelligence Summaries are contained in F. S. Regs., Part II. and the Staff Manual respectively. Title pages will be prepared in manuscript.

Hour, Date, Place	Summary of Events and Information	Remarks and references to Appendices
17-4-15. YPRES.	Dispositions as on previous day. Relieved by 3rd Mons.r Reg.t Battalion returned to YPRES for rest — arrived 2-30 a.m. Casualties:- 1 died of wounds. 2 Wounded.	(a 15-17: K/12. W. 46
18-4-15. YPRES.	Resting.	
19-4-15. YPRES.	Resting	
20-4-15. YPRES.	Resting. YPRES was shelled. — the Battalion moved out into Bivouac in the fields adjoining ST. JEAN.	
21-4-15. ST. JEAN.	Battalion in Bivouac. The troops were moved nearer to ST. JEAN during the night.	
22-4-15. ST. JEAN. 11 a.m.	The Battalion was ordered forward to C21C X Roads with instructions to dig in. Heavy shelling during the day. Very few casualties.	

WAR DIARY or INTELLIGENCE SUMMARY

Army Form C. 2118.

Hour, Date, Place	Summary of Events and Information	Remarks and references to Appendices
23-4-15. C21C. N of St JEAN	Battalion standing to. Heavy shelling. The following order was received at 4-10 p.m on Friday 23-4-15 To 5/K.O.R Lancaster Regt. G.K. 37. Date 23rd "Following has been sent to EAST YORKS and YORK and LANCS. begins –] The 13th BRIGADE crosses by the pontoon bridge at 3 p.m. and advances to the attack at 3-4-5 p.m with the right on the PILCKEM-YPRES road. a.a.a First objective PILCKEM. a.a.a [O.C. EAST YORKS will send an officer at once to report to General Ogowam at Pontoon Bridge C19C. a.a.a EAST YORKS and YORK and LANCS^R will co-operate in this attack East of the PILCKEM-YPRES road, EAST YORKS with left on that road, and maintaining touch with 13th BRIGADE. YORK and LANCS^R will move on the right of the EAST YORKS a.a.a. Two battalions of the 27th Division will co-operate in the attack on the right of the YORK and LANCS^R a.a.a. BUFFS and 3rd MIDDLESEX will hold their present line. a.a.a 5th KING'S OWN ROYAL LANCASTER, less one Company, will follow the attack in Reserve moving with its left on the PILCKEM-YPRES road. a.a.a	

Army Form C. 2118.

WAR DIARY
or
INTELLIGENCE SUMMARY

(Erase heading not required.)

Instructions regarding War Diaries and Intelligence Summaries are contained in F. S. Regs., Part II. and the Staff Manual respectively. Title pages will be prepared in manuscript.

Hour, Date, Place	Summary of Events and Information	Remarks and references to Appendices
23-4-15. C. 21. C. M. of ST JEAN (continued).	(Order continued):- Each Battalion will move on a front of 500 yards a.a. Head-Quarters will remain for the present at WIELTJE where reports should be sent." Lt. Geddes. 3-35 p.m. 5 P.M. The battalion moved for attack - "C" Coy. leading. As they deployed, they were met with heavy shell fire. Immediately they reached their position they came under machine-gun and rifle fire from the front and both flanks. Casualties were numerous from the very outset. The advance was carried out in perfect order, every man pressing forward to the objective. On coming in line with the troops of the attack, they were held up for lack of support. A halt was made and soon men retired or made for himself, even later it was deemed advisable to fall back 1/200 yards and dig in a new line, "A" Coy and a platoon of "D" Coy taking this duty whilst the remainder of the Battalion fell back to its position prior to the commencement of the attack. Casualties:- Officers. 1 killed and 2 died of wounds. Other Ranks. 36 killed. Wounded:- 3 Officers, 144 other ranks. Missing:- 21 other ranks.	

Army Form C. 2118.

WAR DIARY
or
INTELLIGENCE SUMMARY
(Erase heading not required.)

Instructions regarding War Diaries and Intelligence Summaries are contained in F. S. Regs, Part II. and the Staff Manual respectively. Title pages will be prepared in manuscript.

Hour, Date, Place	Summary of Events and Information	Remarks and references to Appendices
24-4-15 C.21.C. N. of ST. JEAN.	Disposition as on previous day. Heavy shelling but only minor casualties.	
25-4-15 C.21.C. N. of ST. JEAN.	Disposition as on previous day. Again, heavy shelling.	
26-4-15 C.21.C. N. of ST. JEAN.	Left for POTIZE at 3 a.m., arriving without further casualties	
27-4-15. POTIZE	The Battalion was ordered to support an attack on C 15. In moving up under a very heavy fire from shell, one shell killed 12 men and wounded 5 others. Dug in, and remained under arms for the rest of the night.	
28-4-15. POTIZE	Similar dispositions as on previous day. Heavy shelling.	
29-4-15. Huts in H.5.	Rest and re-organisation.	
30-4-15 Huts in H.5.	Rest and re-organization	

Michael J Cavendish Green - Lt Col.
O/c. Royal Lancaster Regt

131/5610

1st (Vaughan)
28th Division

1/5th Royal Lancs

Vol IV — 31.5.15

Army Form C. 2118.

5th Kings Own (R. Lanc. Regt.)

WAR DIARY
or
INTELLIGENCE SUMMARY

(Erase heading not required.)

Instructions regarding War Diaries and Intelligence
Summaries are contained in F. S. Regs, Part II.
and the Staff Manual respectively. Title pages
will be prepared in manuscript.

Hour, Date, Place	Summary of Events and Information	Remarks and references to Appendices
May 1st 1915 HUTS H.5.	Rest and re-organization.	
May 2nd { HUTS H.5. / FREZENBERG.	Left Huts in H.5. Went to FREZENBERG, A and D Coys unimproved the fire trenches and occupied them. B and C Coys took over dug-outs in rear of trenches from the Welch Regt. Slightly shelled.	
May 3rd. FREZENBERG.	Heavily shelled. C Coy in morning sent to support RIFLE BRIGADE first heavily from shell fire and got held up. Proceeded on left on road. B Coy attached to EAST YORKS and YORK & LANCS in afternoon. Proceeded on right of road via ZONNEBEKE. Got close to trenches lay down and waited for dark. After dark ordered to dugouts as trenches were to be evacuated.	
May 4th. FREZENBERG.	Still at FREZENBERG. Shelled for 14 hours. A,C, & D. Coys in fire trench. B Coy in dugouts.	
May 5th FREZENBERG	Heavy shelling and casualties correspondingly heavy. Two platoons of B Coy sent up to support fire trench. Relieved by 2 KING'S OWN. Went to HUTS in H.5.	
May 6th. HUTS in H.5.	Rest and re-organization.	

Army Form C. 2118.

WAR DIARY
or
INTELLIGENCE SUMMARY

(Erase heading not required.)

Instructions regarding War Diaries and Intelligence Summaries are contained in F. S. Regs., Part II. and the Staff Manual respectively. Title pages will be prepared in manuscript.

Hour, Date, Place	Summary of Events and Information	Remarks and references to Appendices
May 7th. Huts in H5. {St Jean.	Left Huts and proceeded to dugouts near Brigade Head-Quarters close to ST JEAN.	
May 8th. ST JEAN	Ordered to G.H.Q. lines as supports. Heavily shelled in G.H.Q lines. Ordered to advance to retake trenches that had been lost and also on remainder of 2nd KINGS OWN and 3rd MONMOUTHS. Advanced under heavy shell fire and enfilade fire from maxims placed in a house on NORTH side of POTIJZE – ZONNEBEKE road. Occupied trenches 1300 yards in advance of G.H.Q. lines. Bayonet charge ordered at night which failed.	
May 9th. Huts in H5.	Shelled fairly heavy. Relieved and went to Huts in H5.	
May 10th. Huts in H5.	Brigade made into a composite battalion under COLONEL GOUGH of 3rd MONS. Went to POTIJZE and dug shelter trenches by night.	
May 11th. POTIJZE	Went to G.H.Q lines. Relieved at night, going to bivouac at G.5.	
May 12th. Huts at G.5.	Resting. Moved nearer POPERINGHE.	
May 13th. Near POPERINGHE.	Resting. Ordered to stand to, but orders cancelled. Orders to prepare to move.	

1247 W 3299 200,000 (E) 8/14 J.B.C. & A. Forms/C. 2118/11.

Army Form C. 2118.

WAR DIARY
or
INTELLIGENCE SUMMARY
(Erase heading not required.)

Instructions regarding War Diaries and Intelligence Summaries are contained in F. S. Regs, Part II. and the Staff Manual respectively. Title pages will be prepared in manuscript.

Hour, Date, Place	Summary of Events and Information	Remarks and references to Appendices
May 14th. RYVELD.	Moved by RYVELD. Bus motorbus to STEENVOORDE and marched to RYVELD.	
May 15th. RYVELD.	Rest and re-organization.	
May 16th. RYVELD.	Returned parades for C of E and Wesleyans near billets. For R. Catholics at WINNEZEELE. Inspection by Brigadier, Col MARDEN in afternoon at 3-0 p.m.	
May 17th. RYVELD.	Re-organization and re-equipment.	
May 18th. RYVELD.	As previous day.	
May 19th. RYVELD.	As previous day.	
May 20th. RYVELD.	As previous day.	
May 21st. RYVELD / VLAMERTINGHE	Brigade inspected at WINNEZEELE by General French, who thanked the Brigade for work done in the second battle of YPRES. In afternoon Battalion moved to bivouac near VLAMERTINGHE.	
May 22nd. VLAMERTINGHE	Battalion moved to trenches in I 24 at 4-30 p.m.	
May 23rd. I 24.	Quiet day.	
May 24th. I 24.	Enemy attacked on left with gas. Trenches, supports and dugouts heavily shelled from 2-30 a.m. till 3-0 p.m. Casualties nil p.e.	

Army Form C. 2118.

WAR DIARY
or
INTELLIGENCE SUMMARY

(Erase heading not required.)

Instructions regarding War Diaries and Intelligence Summaries are contained in F. S. Regs., Part II. and the Staff Manual respectively. Title pages will be prepared in manuscript.

Hour, Date, Place	Summary of Events and Information	Remarks and references to Appendices
May 25th. I 34.	Trenches shelled between 3 and 10 a.m. Adjutants & H Qrs heavily shelled. Battalion relieved by YORKSHIRE LIGHT INFANTRY at night. Retired to G.H.Q. line [2nd line]	
May 26th. G.H.Q. line	Heavily shelled. [Shell fell in dugouts at night] Several killed and wounded. Capt. Fawcett rejoined the Battalion	
May 27th. G.H.Q. line	Quiet. Working on repair of G.H.Q. line at night.	
May 28th. G.H.Q. line	Fairly quiet all day. Repaired G.H.Q. line at night.	
May 29th. G.H.Q. line	As on 28th.	
May 30th. G.H.Q. line	As on 29th.	
May 31st. G.H.Q. line	As previous days. Shelled at night. Zeppelin sighted due NORTH travelling WESTWARDS.	

Rupeld.
June 5th 1915.

W.R.H. Dent
Capt. and Adjt.

83rd Bde.
28th Div.

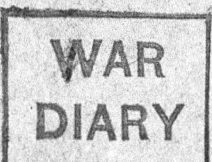

1/5th K.O.R.L.

JUNE

1915

Army Form C. 2118.

WAR DIARY
or
INTELLIGENCE SUMMARY
(Erase heading not required.) 1/5th Batt'n Kings Own (R. Lanc. Regt.)

Instructions regarding War Diaries and Intelligence Summaries are contained in F. S. Regs., Part II. and the Staff Manual respectively. Title pages will be prepared in manuscript.

Hour, Date, Place	Summary of Events and Information	Remarks and references to Appendices
TUESDAY JUNE 1st ZILLEBEKE.	Repairs to G.H.Q. line. Quiet day.	
JUNE 2nd ZILLEBEKE / OUDERDOM H19	Trenches in G.H.Q. line shelled violently from 2 P.M. to 6-15 P.M. Battalion relieved from duty at night; marched to huts in H19 (Sheet 28) near OUDERDOM	
JUNE 3rd OUDERDOM / RYVELD	Battalion left at 2-30 P.M. and marched to billets at RYVELD. Arrived at RYVELD 8-35 P.M.	
JUNE 4th RYVELD.	Rest and re-organisation.	
JUNE 5th RYVELD.	Rest, re-organisation and training. Route march under O.C. Coys. in morning. Parade afternoon Saluting Drill	
JUNE 6th RYVELD	HOLY COMMUNION for C. of ENGLAND MASS " R. CATHOLICS Parade Service for NONCONFORMISTS " " C. of ENGLAND	

Army Form C. 2118.

WAR DIARY
or
INTELLIGENCE SUMMARY

(Erase heading not required.)

1/5th Kings Own (R. Lanc Regt)

Instructions regarding War Diaries and Intelligence Summaries are contained in F.S. Regs., Part II. and the Staff Manual respectively. Title pages will be prepared in manuscript.

Hour, Date, Place	Summary of Events and Information	Remarks and references to Appendices
JUNE 7th RYVELD	Re-organisation & Training. Practice in Entrenching.	
" 8th RYVELD	Battalion marched to MONT-DES-RÉCOLLETS and carried out Rapid Fire Practice. Started 6-30 a.m. Returned 2-30 p.m.	
" 9th RYVELD	Re-organisation and training. Trench digging and Route March.	
" 10th RYVELD	Regtl S.M. Parade 10-0 – 11-0 a.m. Entrenching and Route March [10 miles]. Extended order drill for one hour in afternoon.	
" 11th RYVELD	Morning Battalion went to baths at WINNIZEELE. Trench digging for instruction in afternoon. Officers' class in map-reading at 5-0 p.m. under Major GROGAN [28th Division]. Grenadier platoon formed under Lieut W.M. BRIGGS. Draft of 43 arrived from 2/5 Batn THE KING'S OWN [R. Lanc Regt]	
" 12th RYVELD	Regtl Sergeant Major Parade 10-0 – 10-45 followed by Route march of 9 miles by Coy/o.	
" 13th RYVELD	Divine service for all denominations in morning. Close order drill in afternoon.	

Army Form C. 2118.

WAR DIARY
or
INTELLIGENCE SUMMARY

(Erase heading not required.) 1/5th King's Own (Royal Lancs Regt)

Instructions regarding War Diaries and Intelligence Summaries are contained in F.S. Regs., Part II. and the Staff Manual respectively. Title pages will be prepared in manuscript.

Hour, Date, Place	Summary of Events and Information	Remarks and references to Appendices
JUNE 14th { RYVELD / HUTS M.6.a	Battalion moved from RYVELD to HUTS in M.6.a. [Sheet 28] Trenches filled in during morning.	
" 15th HUTS M.6.a.	Re-organizing and equipping. 9-0 p.m. Practice alarm for the whole Battalion.	
" 16th HUTS M.6.a.	Close order drill and practice in relieving and occupying trenches for instruction of new draft.	
" 17th HUTS M.6.a.	Morning:- Route march about 6 miles. Lectures on "Methods of attack". Afternoon. Battalion Drill.	
" 18th HUTS M.6.a	Close order drill and practice and instruction in repelling attack from trenches. Lectures on "Trench Discipline" by O.C. Corps. Battn. on duty for 24 hours from 6 p.m.	
" 19th HUTS M.6.a	Joint concert with 2nd Battn – WATERLOO DAY. Training. Battn. standing to until 6-0 p.m.	
" 20th { HUTS M.6.a / LOCRE	Battalion moved to bivouacs near LOCRE	

Army Form C. 2118.

WAR DIARY
or
INTELLIGENCE SUMMARY
(Erase heading not required.)

1/5th King's Own (Lancaster Regt.)

Hour, Date, Place		Summary of Events and Information	Remarks and references to Appendices
JUNE 21st.	LOCRE.	Training. Fatigues to trenches at night.	
" 22nd	LOCRE.	Training. Baths at WESTOUTRE. Fatigues to trenches at night	
" 23rd	LOCRE.	Training. Fatigues to trenches at night. "D" Coy proceeded to trenches with 1st Battn. KING'S OWN. YORKSe. LIGHT INFANTRY.	
" 24th	LOCRE / LA CLYTTE	Battalion moved to Huts near LA CLYTTE. Transport to M 11. c [Sheet 28] Working party to trenches at night.	
" 25th.	LA CLYTTE	Training	
" 26th.	LA CLYTTE	Training. Bath provides working party fatigue parties to the trenches	
" 27	LA CLYTTE	Training. Baths at WESTOUTRE. Divine service for all denominations. Fatigue parties at night.	

Army Form C. 2118.

WAR DIARY
or
INTELLIGENCE SUMMARY

(Erase heading not required.)

1/5th The Kings Own (Relance Regt)

Hour, Date, Place	Summary of Events and Information	Remarks and references to Appendices
JUNE 28th LA CLYTTE	Training. Route March. Working party to trenches at night.	
" 29th LA CLYTTE	Training Working party (83rd) and for trenches at night. Working party "A" Coy relieved "D" Coy in trenches H1 & H2 (KEMMEL) [VIERSTRAAT]	
" 30th LA CLYTTE	Training "C" Coy went to trenches H5 [KEMMEL VIERSTRAAT] at night to take over – attached to 1st EAST YORKS REGT. Transport inspection by Commanding Officer.	

July 1st 1915.

Ed. R. Cadman Major
and Commanding Officer

83rd Bde.
28th Div.

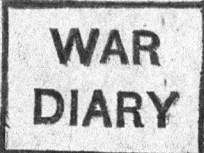

1/5th K. O. R. L.

J U L Y

1 9 1 5

Army Form C. 2118.

WAR DIARY
or
INTELLIGENCE SUMMARY

(Erase heading not required.)   5th King's Own Royal Lancaster Regt.

Instructions regarding War Diaries and Intelligence Summaries are contained in F. S. Regs., Part II. and the Staff Manual respectively. Title pages will be prepared in manuscript.

Hour, Date, Place		Summary of Events and Information	Remarks and references to Appendices
1915			
1st July	LA CLYTTE.	Training.	
2nd July	LA CLYTTE.	Route march. Fatigues to trenches	
3rd July	LA CLYTTE.	General training. Competition between 2nd King's Own & 5th King's Own transport sections.	
4th July	LA CLYTTE.	Training. Divine service for all denominations. Fatigues to trenches at night	
5th July	LA CLYTTE.	Training. Brigade Guards furnished by "D" Coy. Various Brigade fatigues found. Working and carrying parties to trenches. B and D Coys relieved A & C [ventilin 29th June & 30th June respectively] in trenches H1. 2. + H5.	
6th July	LA CLYTTE.	General training. Inspection of arms and equipment. Brigade Guard [ventilin on 5th by D Coy] from Coy. in trenches	
7th July	LA CLYTTE.	General training and reorganisation. Baths at RENINGHELST for A and C Coys.	
8th July	LA CLYTTE.	Training. A and C Coys provide 50 men each for Brigade Fatigues	

Army Form C. 2118.

WAR DIARY
or
INTELLIGENCE SUMMARY

(Erase heading not required.)

5th Kings Own [Royal Lancr Regt]

Hour, Date, Place	Summary of Events and Information	Remarks and references to Appendices
9th July LA CLYTTE	Training. Fatigues and carrying parties for trenches at night.	
10th July LA CLYTTE	General training and re-equipping. Fatigues/Ration parties to trenches at night	
11th July LA CLYTTE	Training. Divine Service for all denominations. A and C Coys provide Brigade Guards. Baths for specialists at LA CLYTTE	
12th July LA CLYTTE	Training. A and C Coys relieve B & D Coys. Occupy all K trenches less K1 and K3, also S.P. 12 & 13, attached 2nd East Yorks. Also M.G. team attached to KING'S OWN YORKS LIGHT INFANTRY	
13th July LA CLYTTE	Training. Inspection of arms and equipment B and D Coys. Baths at LA CLYTTE for B & D Coys.	
14th July LA CLYTTE	Training & Contretiring. Lt. MANSFIELD & Sergt WRIGHT posted to M.G. Section.	
15th July LA CLYTTE	Training. Smoke helmets sprayed.	
16th July LA CLYTTE	General training. Baths at LA CLYTTE.	

Army Form C. 2118.

WAR DIARY
or
INTELLIGENCE SUMMARY
(Erase heading not required.)

5th Kings Own Rgt

Hour, Date, Place		Summary of Events and Information	Remarks and references to Appendices
1915.			
17th July	LA CLYTTE	Training. A and C return from trenches.	
18th July	LA CLYTTE	Divine service for all denominations. Training. Baths for A and C at LA CLYTTE. Major CADMAN and Capt EAVES reconnoitre 'L' trenches	
19th July	LA CLYTTE	Training. Carrying and working parties 1 + 4 for trenches. Capt EAVES, Capt FAWCETT and Lt MILNE's reconnoitre Subsidiary line. Lt Milne's appointed Adjutant as from May 5th 9.5.	
20th July	LA CLYTTE	General training for whole Battalion. Col. HARRISS Lt MANSFIELD reconnoitre new line of trenches all "L" trenches also K2 & LK3 [Kemmel, Left Sector]	
21st July	{LA CLYTTE / KEMMEL}	Training. Battalion goes into trenches at KEMMEL, LEFT SECTOR. Occupy all 'L' trenches with K3 and K2b. D'Coy. [Two +6 men attached to A.B & Coys. in trenches] at Battn Head Quarters YORK HOUSE. M. Gun teams in L5, L6 and L7.	
22nd July	KEMMEL	Disposition as above. Situation quiet. Coy general fatigue at night to trenches	

Army Form C. 2118.

WAR DIARY
or
INTELLIGENCE SUMMARY
(Erase heading not required.)

5th Kings Own [Royal Lanc Regt.]

Hour, Date, Place	Summary of Events and Information	Remarks and references to Appendices
23rd July, KEMMEL	As yesterday. Situation normal. Trenches improved generally.	
24th July, KEMMEL	Dispositions as before. Officers 7 R. Yorks and 6th Dorsets [NEW ARMY] reconnoitre trenches. 2 Platoons of each above Regt. go up to LEFT SECTOR for instruction. L4 and L5 shelled with HE and common shell. Casualties 1 [Kings Own 5th July 3rd [3]] in K2a. [Your Hance in SANDBAG VILLA relieved by 2nd Kings Own R.L.R.] Wire entanglements in LEFT sector patrolled and examined. Repaired and strengthened where necessary.	
25th July, KEMMEL	As yesterday. Platoons of New Army relieved by same units. Trenches reconnoitred by officers of 7th YORKS and 6th DORSETS by day. Slight shelling of LEFT SECTOR from S.E. Common shell. Situation generally quiet. Great activity enemy planes. Trenches generally strengthened and drained. C. Trenches improved. Reconnoitring patrol found enemy working on wire.	

Army Form C. 2118.

WAR DIARY
or
INTELLIGENCE SUMMARY

(Erase heading not required.)

5th Kings Own [Volunteer Regt?]

Instructions regarding War Diaries and Intelligence Summaries are contained in F. S. Regs., Part II. and the Staff Manual respectively. Title pages will be prepared in manuscript.

Hour, Date, Place	Summary of Events and Information	Remarks and references to Appendices
26th July KEMMEL	Trenches shelled. Casualties O.R. killed 1 [1st Yorks] O.R. wounded 5 [3, 5th King's Own, 1 York & Lancs, 1 1st Yorks]. Platoons of New Army relieved by ours who. Two enemy flares brought down. A'cal activity by own & hostile artillery directed by planes. Civilians prohibited EAST of NEUVE EGLISE – YPRES Road.	
27th July KEMMEL	Disposition as before. Trenches further improved and traverses built. Patrols reported enemy working on parapets twice. Casualties Nil.	
28th July KEMMEL	Situation generally quiet. C. Trenches defences & parades rebuilt. New Army Platoons relieved by 6th DORSETS and EAST YORKS. [2nd King's Own Respectively relieved by K.O.Y.L.I.] Casualties. O.R. wounded 8. [3 5th King's Own, 4 6th Dorsets 1 7th Yorks]	
29th July KEMMEL	Disposition as before. Trenches sandbagged where breached by enemy shell fire. Wire strengthened along whole front. Renewed in places where weak.	

1247   W 8299   200,000   (E)   8/14   J.B.C. & A.   Forms/C. 2118/11.

WAR DIARY or **INTELLIGENCE SUMMARY**
(Erase heading not required.)

Army Form C. 2118.

5th Kings Own [Reference Regt.]

Hour, Date, Place	Summary of Events and Information	Remarks and references to Appendices
29th July KEMMEL (continued).	Patrol discovered enemy working on farm Emplacement in front of haraises [Bearings taken and forwarded to 83rd Bgde.mgm.Gp.]	
3-30 pm	Our heavy artillery bombarded HOSPICE rear of enemy line. Potun only left standing. Situation Normal. Casualties O.R. killed 1. York Hans.	
30th July KEMMEL	Dispositions as before. Sandbags built into parapets. Trenches generally improved. Parados repaired. Two working parties with R.E. working on L.I. Nevr. Situation quiet. Casualties O.R. wounded 3 (York Hans). Battalion relieved at night by 1st Kings Own Yorkshire Light Infy with 2 Coys 5th Brigade (New Army) attached. Relief completed 11-15 pm. On relief battalion proceeded to bivouacs at SCHERPENBERG bivouacs.	
31st July SCHERPENBERG BIVOUACS.	Rest and reorganisation. Baths at WESTOUTRE. Brigade band played evening.	

Ed. C. Podmore Major
Commdg. 5th Kings Own [Regt.]

Operation Orders by Major Cadman Comm'g 5th King's Own
21-7-15.

1. The Battalion will move to trenches tonight, parade at 7-0 p.m.

2. Disposition & Order of March as follows.

TRENCH	GARRISON		COY.		OFFICERS
L7 Left	37	}	B		Capt. Deed
L7 Right	32	}			Lt Parkinson
L6	34				
L5	71	}	A	97	Capt Fawcett
L4	36	}	D	10	Lt. Sunnucks
L3	32	}			
L2	36	}	C	112	Capt Caves
L1	11	}	D	3	Lt Biggs
K3	36				Lt Bell
K2b	27		D Coy.		Sgt Smith

YORK HOUSE D Coy. less 40   Capt Harrison
L5, L6 & L7 Machine G. Sect. No 1, 2 & 3. Lt. Mansfield

3. Signallers Sgt Heaton & 4 wiremen will report at Head Quarters 2nd King's Own at 11-0 a.m. Remainder of Signallers will be at barrier KEMMEL — LA CLYTTE road at 2-30 p.m.
They will be met by a guide from 2nd King's Own

4. Stretcher Bearers. 2 S.B. will be attached to each Coy. and 2 to Head Quarters. S.B. will march off with the Coys they are attached to.

5. Taking Over. One senior N.C.O. from each Coy. will report to Head Qrs 2nd Kings Own before 3 p.m. to take over trenches and meet the Coy. at barrier with guides.

6. On relief, O/C. Coys. will report to Head Qrs. by wire when their Coys. are in.
   The M.G. officer will also report.

7. Smoke Helmets. O/C. Coys. will see that their men have two smoke helmets or one smoke helmet and one respirator. The helmet will be carried round the neck & second smoke helmet or respirator in haversack.

8. Sand-bags Rations & Water. Every man will carry one day's rations and three sandbags. Water bottles will be filled.

9. Kitchens will be ready to move at 5-30 p.m.

10. All blankets & shelters to be ready for loading at 5-p.m.

11. Canteen will be dismantled and barrels returned at 3 p.m.

12. Furniture. Officers Mess Boxes & officers kits will be ready for loading at 5-30 p.m.

13. Trench store indents will be at Hd. Qrs. at 7 a.m.

14. Cpl. Preston will act as Sanitary Cpl. in the trenches.

15. Regt'l. S-Major Nelson will proceed to Hd Qrs 2nd. King's Own to take over ammunition and trench stores at YORK HOUSE & SANDBAG VILLA by 3·0 pm.

16. One guide from each Coy. will report to Battalion Head Quarters.

83rd Bde.
28th Div.

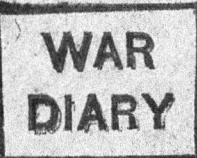

1/5th K. O. R. L.

A U G U S T

1 9 1 5

Army Form C. 2118.

WAR DIARY
or
INTELLIGENCE SUMMARY

(Erase heading not required.)

Instructions regarding War Diaries and Intelligence Summaries are contained in F. S. Regs., Part II. and the Staff Manual respectively. Title pages will be prepared in manuscript.

Hour, Date, Place	Summary of Events and Information	Remarks and references to Appendices
	War Diary	
	August 1915	
	5th Bn. The King's Own. Rl. Lanc. Regt.	

Army Form C. 2118.

WAR DIARY
or
INTELLIGENCE SUMMARY

5th Bn. THE KING'S OWN (R. LANC. REGT.)

(Erase heading not required.)

Instructions regarding War Diaries and Intelligence Summaries are contained in F. S. Regs., Part II. and the Staff Manual respectively. Title pages will be prepared in manuscript.

Hour, Date, Place	Summary of Events and Information	Remarks and references to Appendices
Aug. 1st SCHERPENBERG bivouacs	General training. Divine Service all denominations. Fatigue party 4 officers 200 men to work on SUBSIDIARY LINE [KEMMEL – LEFT SECTOR].	
do.	General training. Both used range at SCHERPENBERG for M. Gun practice and Musketry.	
Aug. 3rd do.	Training. B and D Coys moved to trenches at KEMMEL [RIGHT SECTOR] attached to 13th York & Lanc't Regt. Garrison H2 H3 & H5. Machine Gun teams in H3 and S.P.12, 6 signallers, 6 stretcher bearers in each trench. A & C provide two fatigue parties at night (working party 50, Sapping " 50)	
Aug. 4th SCHERPENBERG LOCRE	Remainder of battalion and cyclists (A & C coys hdqrs) move from SCHERPENBERG to LOCRE at 10-30 a.m. 4 p.m. Exhibition of Capt. WEST'S hand-throwing machine at SCHERPENBERG. All grenadier platoons in Brigade attend for instruction.	

Army Form C. 2118.

WAR DIARY
or
INTELLIGENCE SUMMARY
(Erase heading not required.)

Instructions regarding War Diaries and Intelligence Summaries are contained in F. S. Regs., Part II. and the Staff Manual respectively. Title pages will be prepared in manuscript.

Hour, Date, Place		Summary of Events and Information	Remarks and references to Appendices
Aug 5th	LOCRE	B & D coys in trenches. Morning – general training A & C. Afternoon A & C MG section on SCHERPENBERG, Musketry. At night, following carrying parties detached C coy 80 A 70 MG Section 13 S Bearers 2 Casualties: O.R. wounded 3.	
Aug 6th	LOCRE	Training. Inspection of Arms & Equipment. Instruction in Bayonet fighting.	
Aug 7th	LOCRE	B & D in trenches. General training.	
Aug 8th	do	Parades arse for all communications. Instruction of Arms. General training.	
Aug 9th	do	B & D in trenches. Disposition as on 3rd Aug. Head qr & section, A & 16 coys on SCHERPENBERG RANGE. Casualties O.R. killed 2. wounded 3. Heavy bombardment due NORTH in YPRES district [HOOGE] Battalion stood to from 3 a.m. to 6·0 a.m. [B & D in trenches report hearing cannonade from the artillery supporting their trenches. Possibly to distract enemy attention]	

Army Form C. 2118.

5th Bn. THE KING'S OWN (R. LANC. REGT.)

WAR DIARY
or
INTELLIGENCE SUMMARY

(Erase heading not required.)

Hour, Date, Place		Summary of Events and Information	Remarks and references to Appendices
Aug 10th	LOCRE	General training. A and C Coys relieve B & D Coys in H2, H3 and H5. Machine gun detachment relieve detachment in H3. Extract from Battn. Opr. Orders a. Coys & M.G. detachments parade 7-15 p.m. move off 7-45 p.m. They will not pass the Jonction KEMMEL – LACLYTTE road before 8-30 p.m. b. Captn Fawcett will be in command of the party. The twenty will come under the command of the O.C. Coy Coys at Relief. c. Necessary reconnaissance of trenches will be carried out in the afternoon.			Carried out by Officers of A & C Coys.
Aug 11th	LOCRE { SCHERPENBERG }	Half Battn. B & D Coys. Headquarters & details move to — M 11. c. 4. 5. Troops M 17 c. 6. 5. Transport } Sheet 28 all to be clear of LOCRE by 2-0 p.m.	
Aug 13th	SCHERPENBERG	General training. B & D Coys think Section Musketry practice on SCHERPENBERG. Carrying party at night of 90 men.	

Army Form C. 2118.

5th Bn. THE KING'S OWN (R. LANC. REGT.)

WAR DIARY
or
INTELLIGENCE SUMMARY
(Erase heading not required.)

Instructions regarding War Diaries and Intelligence Summaries are contained in F. S. Regs., Part II. and the Staff Manual respectively. Title pages will be prepared in manuscript.

Hour, Date, Place	Summary of Events and Information	Remarks and references to Appendices
Aug. 13th SCHERPENBERG	General training. A & C Coys (attached to 2nd Kings Own who relieved 1st York & Lancs) relieved by two Coys. 7th Leicester (S. Battalion) KEMMEL - Regt relief. On relief they rejoin Battalion in bivouacs (extract from Brigade Ops Orders 61. On night 13/14 Aug. after command of 6th Leicester Regt. a. The two Coys 5th Kings Own attached to 2nd Kings Own will rejoin the Headquarters of their Battalion.	
Aug. 14th do	B & D Coys general training. A & C " Inspection of Arms and Equipment.	
Aug. 15th do	Divine Service for all denominations (extract from Battn Orders No 4. A and C Coys. will relieve two Coys. of 6th Leicester Regt. attached to 2nd Kings Own in H2, H3 and H5 tonight.	
Aug. 16th do	a. General training. b. Musketry on SCHERPENBERG range. Captain Leith Manifield and Parkinson reconnoitre G.A., G.aa, H1, 2, 3, 4 and NEW SAP in the afternoon. Casualties O.R. killed one, wounded two.	

Army Form C. 2118.

5th. Bn. THE KING'S OWN (R. LANC. REGT.)

WAR DIARY
or
INTELLIGENCE SUMMARY

(Erase heading not required.)

Instructions regarding War Diaries and Intelligence Summaries are contained in F.S. Regs., Part II. and the Staff Manual respectively. Title pages will be prepared in manuscript.

Hour, Date, Place	Summary of Events and Information	Remarks and references to Appendices
Aug. 17th. SCHERPENBERG	The rest of Battn. Band D Coys. form A and C trenches. Extract from Op. Orders to 5th Bde. 8th Brigade. 1. 1/6th Aug. 1st "My Jane" will relieve 2 Kings Own Regt. in present Right Sector and 5th Kings Own in H5. 2. 5th Kings Own will post two M.G. in S.P. 12 & 1 "My Jane" and depute 25 men in H5, who will come under orders of "My Jane". 3. The 5th Kings Own will take over from the Northumberland Fusiliers the following trenches G.4, G.4a, NEW SAP, H1, SP.11. The garrison in H2 and H3 will remain as at present. 4. The Headquarters of the 5th Kings Own will be at Stella KEMMEL CHATEAU 5. On completion of relief 83rd Brigade front will be divided into three sectors:- RIGHT SECTOR 5th Kings Own CENTRE " 1st York and Lancaster LEFT " 1st K.O.Y. Light Infantry. Relief complete 11-50 pm. Disposition of troops G.4.a. 1 officer 50 men. H3 1 officer 54 men G.4. 1 " 39 " NEW SAP 1 " 73 " H1. 1 " 57 " S.P.11 1 " 43 " H2. 1 " 67 " 25 men in H5 attached 1st York & Lanc."	

Army Form C. 2118.

WAR DIARY
or
INTELLIGENCE SUMMARY
(Erase heading not required.)

Instructions regarding War Diaries and Intelligence Summaries are contained in F. S. Regs., Part II. and the Staff Manual respectively. Title pages will be prepared in manuscript.

Hour, Date, Place	Summary of Events and Information	Remarks and references to Appendices
Aug 19th (continued) KEMMEL [RIGHT SECTOR]	Advance Trench in front of H1 and G4. *[sketch map showing trench layout with labels: MAGNETIC NORTH, NEW SAP, H1A, H GRENADES, H1, WELL, RUIN, to G4 Gap, to H5, bomber, C.T.]* Work done to dawn 18th. Parapets built in H3 and traverses reinforced where damaged by whizzbangs. C.T. between H1 and H5 indurated. Wire in front of whole sector improved.	

DUGOUTS
L   LATRINE.
S   SPRAYER.

WAR DIARY or INTELLIGENCE SUMMARY

(Erase heading not required.)

Army Form C. 2118.

8th Bn. THE KING'S OWN (R. LANC. REGT.)

Hour, Date, Place	Summary of Events and Information	Remarks and references to Appendices
Aug 18th. KEMMEL [RIGHT SECTOR]	Casualties to form O.R wounded one. Enemy Work. Evening patrols report activity on enemy front. They were filling and placing sandbags, and generally improving trenches. O.C. H3 trench reported enemy mining under right flank of H3. Mining officer from T3 investigated. Reported that no damage threatened. Enemy wire reported to be low but of great depth, uniformly good.	
Aug 19th. do.	Disposition as before. Work done to dawn. Trenches cleaned, drained and generally improved. Sandbags filled and built in. Banquette raised. C.T. and parapets improved. Enemy strengthening wire in W area. Unusual number of flares sent up, apparently from opposite patrol unable to discover reason. Patrol located a M.G. on emplacement where M.G. played on "V.C." road. 62nd Artillery informed and opened fire. Hun reported silenced. Pos. of gun. N 24. d. 4. 7 x (hut 2.8 x -x-x-x-x-x-	in M.24.d.4.7

H3 TRENCH.

Army Form C. 2118.

5th. Bn. THE KING'S OWN (R. LANC. REGT.)

WAR DIARY
or
INTELLIGENCE SUMMARY

(Erase heading not required.)

Hour, Date, Place	Summary of Events and Information	Remarks and references to Appendices
Aug 19th. KEMMEL RIGHT SECTOR (continued)	Casualties Nil.	
Aug 20th. do	Situation. Normal on the whole. Disposition of troops as before. Work done. G+t G+a Parapets traversed retained. New latrine trench NEW SAP] Dugouts made. Parapet retained. Sandbags refilled and H.1.2.+3 } built in. Wire retained. Sick Wastage. O.R. three. Casualties. O.R. 2 { one self inflicted, one accidentally wounded. General. Machine Gun in M.2 + d.4.7 Sheet 28 referred to in Sheet 7 is either undamaged or has been replaced by another. O.K. trench reports that gun fired several bursts at varying intervals on Aug. 19th (evening) 63rd Battery informed. No further action taken. Brig-Gen. Ravenshaw. E.O.C. 83rd Brigade visited Battn Orrs and also made a tour of trenches.	

Army Form C. 2118.

WAR DIARY
or
INTELLIGENCE SUMMARY
(Erase heading not required.)

Instructions regarding War Diaries and Intelligence Summaries are contained in F. S. Regs., Part II. and the Staff Manual respectively. Title pages will be prepared in manuscript.

Hour, Date, Place	Summary of Events and Information	Remarks and references to Appendices
Aug. 31st KEMMEL RIGHT SECTOR G4a & G4	Work done to dawn. Parapets built. "Slip" trenches constructed. Wire improved generally. Sandbags filled and parapet re-topped. Broad traverse built in NEW SAP. Wastage O.R. two Casualties O.R. one slightly at duty. T.D. TRENCH DUMP M.G. MACHINE GUN T TELEPHONE L LATRINE	Also called "SLIT" trenches. [Protection against Artillery fire]

Army Form C. 2118.

6TH. BN. THE KING'S OWN (R. LANC. REGT.)

WAR DIARY
or
INTELLIGENCE SUMMARY

(Erase heading not required.)

Instructions regarding War Diaries and Intelligence Summaries are contained in F. S. Regs., Part II. and the Staff Manual respectively. Title pages will be prepared in manuscript.

Hour, Date, Place	Summary of Events and Information	Remarks and references to Appendices
Aug 21st KEMMEL [RIGHT SECTOR] [Continued]	6 O.6 83rd Brigade visited aspm trenches Head Quarters Right Sector. Officers 3rd Monmouth Regt [TF] reconnoitred Right Sector trenches. 10pm 1/83rd Bde wire. Heavy Artillery will fire on MESSINES TOWER at 5pm. Result of bombardment not communicated. Extract from 83rd Bde Op. Orders 6A. 1. On night 22/23 Aug. 3rd Monmouth Regt will relieve 5th Kings Own in Right Sector and their 2.5 men in H5. 2. M.G. teams of 5th Kings Own (nat guns) in NEW SAP and H3 will be relieved 3. On relief 5th Kings Own will proceed to bivouacs at SCHERPENBERG.	
August 22nd	do. Work done to dawn. Parapets, traverses, and banquettes repaired. Trenches cleaned and drained. Trench gratings relaid C.T. deepened. Wire strengthened and deepened where necessary. Listening patrols sent out. NO new movements apparent on enemy front. Enemy strengthening wire. Working parties fired out by enemy. Rapid fire opened by us. Casualties N.L. O Ranks one. Sick Wastage O Ranks one.	

Army Form C. 2118.

WAR DIARY
or
INTELLIGENCE SUMMARY
(Erase heading not required.)

Instructions regarding War Diaries and Intelligence Summaries are contained in F. S. Regs., Part II. and the Staff Manual respectively. Title pages will be prepared in manuscript.

Hour, Date, Place	Summary of Events and Information	Remarks and references to Appendices
Aug 22nd KEMMEL [RIGHT SECTOR]	**General.** Tests were carried out in all trenches at 2 p.m. as per 83rd Brigade B.M.A. 392 i.e. battling an intensity to support infantry. Times taken as follows:- G4a. 60 seconds. H1, 2, +3 40 " } MAXIMUM NEW SAP 20 " } TIMES. Times were communicated to Brigade HQrs. **Relief.** Relief (by 3rd Worc. Regt) complete by 10-30 p.m. Detail of Ammunition Expended to worn daily:	

	G4a	G4H	NEW SAP	H1. H2. H3	SP 11	TOTAL
Aug 18	905	NIL	800	560	NIL	2265
" 19	800	"	900	230	"	1930
" 20	580	"	650	540	"	1770
" 21	980	"	570	680	"	2230
" 22	475	"	590	1130	"	2195
	3740		3510	3140		10,390

Total rounds expended 10,390.

Army Form C. 2118.

5th Bn. THE KING'S OWN (R. LANC. REGT.)

WAR DIARY
or
INTELLIGENCE SUMMARY

(Erase heading not required.)

Hour, Date, Place	Summary of Events and Information	Remarks and references to Appendices
Aug 23rd SCHERPENBERG	General training. Inspection of Arms and Equipment. Casualties to NOON Killed O.R. one	
Aug 24th do.	Training. Baths at LOCRE. Working parties of 270 men at 9 a.m. and 2 p.m. Carrying party at night for 2/1st Northumbrian Field Coy. R.E. 140 men.	
Aug 25th do	Baths at WESTOUTRE Sick Wastage Officers 2. Capt W. Rushead. " L. L. Milnes. 2nd Lieuts R.A. Hyatt Pryor. Posted to 5th Kings Own Regt. " H. Boys Stones from " A.M. Lunya " H.A. Prefford 10th Service Battn King's Own Regt " R.H. Kinear	

Army Form C. 2118.

5th Bn. THE KING'S OWN (R. LANC. REGT.)

WAR DIARY
or
INTELLIGENCE SUMMARY

(Erase heading not required.)

Instructions regarding War Diaries and Intelligence Summaries are contained in F. S. Regs., Part II. and the Staff Manual respectively. Title pages will be prepared in manuscript.

Hour, Date, Place	Summary of Events and Information	Remarks and references to Appendices
Aug. 26th. SCHERPENBERG	General training. Bayonet fighting & Coy. drill. Lieut Oops - posted to 5th King's Own from 3rd King's Own Regt. " Gardner " " " 10th " " " " Harrold " " " " " " " Cottell " " " " " " " Monks " " " 10th Staffordshire Regt. Enemy planes showing great activity during afternoon and evening.	
Aug. 27th. do	Working parties 7 officers and 290 men for Brigade purposes, morning, afternoon and evening. (Evening party cancelled at 4.30 p.m.)	
Aug. 29th. do	General training in morning. Received from Operation Orders by Brig-Gen H.H.S. Ravenshaw 83rd Brigade. a. On night 28/29 Aug. 5th King's Own will relieve 3rd Worc. Regt. in Right Sector (KEMMEL) and the machine guns of 1st K.O.Y.L. Infy and 2nd King's Own.	

Army Form C. 2118.

(In M. THE KING'S OWN (R. LANC. REG.))

WAR DIARY
or
INTELLIGENCE SUMMARY
(Erase heading not required.)

Instructions regarding War Diaries and Intelligence Summaries are contained in F.S. Regs., Part II. and the Staff Manual respectively. Title pages will be prepared in manuscript.

Hour, Date, Place	Summary of Events and Information	Remarks and references to Appendices
Aug. 28th. SCHERPENBERG.	b. Relieving units will have drawn No's 6 & 8 (?) at 7-15 p.m. c. Completion of relief wired to this office. [Relief complete 10-10 p.m.]	
Aug 29th KEMMEL [RIGHT SECTOR]	Little work was possible owing to relief. Situation normal. Such wastage. O.R. one. Casualties nil. Capt Fawcett O.C. 'B' Coy inspected all the trenches in daylight etc. He reported them good though several want deepening. The enemy wire refusal uniformly good. Enemy reconstructing parapets in places with outward slope – glacis – to lessen damage by shell fire.	For all trenches see Plan Q.

SECTION GERMAN TRENCH SHOWING GLACIS SLOPE

← TO ENGLISH LINES.

Army Form C. 2118.

WAR DIARY
or
INTELLIGENCE SUMMARY
(Erase heading not required.)

Instructions regarding War Diaries and Intelligence Summaries are contained in F.S. Regs., Part II. and the Staff Manual respectively. Title pages will be prepared in manuscript.

Hour, Date, Place	Summary of Events and Information	Remarks and references to Appendices
Aug 30th KEMMEL [RIGHT SECTOR]	**Work done to date:-** a. Parapet and traverses retained and fresh filled sandbags used for re-topping. b. All C.T. in Right Sector were cleaned and drained. c. Wire was strengthened along whole of Right Sector front especially front of H1, 2, 3 & G4a **Patrols** listening patrols heard nothing unusual to report. The advanced to within 15 yds of enemy wire which they reported good, though kept but very deep and generally in a good state of repair. The ground between German trenches and G4a and H1a (NEW SAP) is reported clean. **Sick Wastage** Nil. **Situation** (10 NOON) Normal. Fresh N.W. breeze **General.** Very quiet day. No heavy artillery unusual. Few "whizzbangs" only fired.	

16.

Army Form C. 2118.

WAR DIARY
or
INTELLIGENCE SUMMARY
(Erase heading not required.)

Instructions regarding War Diaries and Intelligence Summaries are contained in F. S. Regs., Part II. and the Staff Manual respectively. Title pages will be prepared in manuscript.

Hour, Date, Place	Summary of Events and Information	Remarks and references to Appendices
Aug. 31st. KEMMEL [RIGHT SECTOR]	**Work done** All along sector the travalets were generally strengthened and reducible where necessary. Special attention devoted to cleaning + drainage of both fire, support, and communication trenches. The slit trenches were deepened, and a new C.T. dug from G4a to listening post infront of wire. Several parties went in reconnaissance of enemy wire. **Patrols** 1st Party. Enemy wire very good and apparently recently repaired. It is strong and no apparent gaps or weak places were observed. The wire was laid on stakes 3'6" high, the stakes being 6 feet apart and six stakes deep (as diagram). There were no knife rests and there was no wire between our wire and the enemy	

→ TO OUR LINES

Army Form C. 2118.

WAR DIARY
or
INTELLIGENCE SUMMARY
(Erase heading not required.)

Instructions regarding War Diaries and Intelligence Summaries are contained in F. S. Regs., Part II. and the Staff Manual respectively. Title pages will be prepared in manuscript.

Hour, Date, Place	Summary of Events and Information	Remarks and references to Appendices
Aug. 31st KEMMEL [RIGHT SECTOR]	Second Party:— Germans were very good. Consists of long and short stakes alternately placed with wire between as diagram [sketch] Several gaps made by our artillery, not repaired. No 'gates were seen A third party was sent out but encountered a German patrol in front of our "Fire Rest". No observation was therefore possible. Further reconnaissance will be made by this party. Situation ——— Normal. Moderate breeze from North West. Sick Wastage ——— O. Ranks two. [diarrhoea and pneumonia]. Casualties ——— O. Ranks one. Pte. left forearm fractured radius.	

Army Form C. 2118.

WAR DIARY
or
INTELLIGENCE SUMMARY

(Erase heading not required.)

Instructions regarding War Diaries and Intelligence Summaries are contained in F. S. Regs., Part II. and the Staff Manual respectively. Title pages will be prepared in manuscript.

Hour, Date, Place	Summary of Events and Information	Remarks and references to Appendices
Aug. 31st KEMMEL [RIGHT SECTOR]	General. Quiet day on the whole. New S.A.P - H1a - reports greater activity in artillery fire on both sides. H.1.a. rather heavily shelled - whizzbangs - during the afternoon. No material damage done.	

Aug. 31st 1915.

Ed. P. Cadman Major
Commanding 5th Bn. The King's Own
Royal Lancaster Regt.

Operation Orders No 2
by
Major E. Cadman, Comdg.
Comdg 5th Kings Own (R.L.R.)
Tuesday 3-8-15

ref sheet 28

1. B. D. Cos & 1 & 2 machine gun detachments will march to the trenches tonight to relieve 7 Cheshire Regt.

   Party will be attached to the 1 York & Lanc. Regt.

   B. D. Cos under Capt. Reed will parade @ 7 p.m. & march off @ 7-50 in rear of B. Coy York & Lanc.

   Machine gun teams will report to Lt. Gribben with limber @ 7.10 p.m.

   Companies will halt for 5 minutes en route.

2. Guides will be provided @ Barrier N 20 b 8.7.

3. Lt. Parkinson with O.Sh's. for B. D. Cos will proceed to the trenches @ 4 p.m. to take over trench stores.

4. O.C. Cos will report relief
complete by wire to Hdqrs. York L.

5. Men will carry 2 sandbags per
man, one days rations & water
bottles filled.

6 Signallers.
    3 Signallers for H 2
         do   H 3
will report to Adjutant 1 York L.
@ 1-15 ready to move off.

7. Stretcher Bearers.
    2 Stretcher Bearers will be
attached to each trench.

8 Minimum garrisons are as follow

D Coy { H 2   60 men 2 S.Bs. 3 Signallers
       { H 3   45   "   do   do.
B. Coy   H 5   75   "   do
         H 3   1 Machine gun
         S.P. 12   do.

    Two guides from B Coy.
will report as orderlies to Hdqrs.
Right Sector. ROSSEGNOL ESTAMINET.

9. Capt Deeb, Lt Manspeed & Sgt Heaton will render a marching out state to the Adjutant on form attached.

(sd.) G.C. Milnes
Capt. Adjt.
5th King's Own (R.L.R.)

3-8-15

Copy No. 1 War Diary
     2 Capt Deeb
     3   Harris
     4 Lt Hodgkinson

Copy No. 1

"Operation Orders No. 3
by
Major Cadman
Cmdg. 5th Bn. The Kings Own (R.L.R.)
10-8-15

1. A & C Cos will relieve B & D Cos in H2, H3, & H5 trenches tonight.
   No. 3 Machine Gun detachment will relieve detachment in H3.
   No. 4 Machine Gun detachment will relieve detachment in S.P.12

2. Companies & M.G. detachments will parade @ 7-15 pm & move off @ 7-45 pm. They will not pass the Barrier on KEMMEL - LA CLYTTE ROAD before 8-30 pm.

3. Three signallers will relieve signallers in H2 trench & 3 signallers will relieve signallers in H3 trench. Signallers will relieve in trenches before 3pm. They will report relief complete by wire to Hdqrs. YORK & LANCS.

4. Two Stretcher Bearers will proceed with each of the three garrisons H2, H3, H5.

5. C.S.Ms. will proceed to trenches @ 2pm. to take over trench stores.

6. Water bottles will be filled, one days rations & two sandbags per man will be carried.

7. Capt. Fawcett will be in charge of the party. Party will be attached to the YORK & LANC. REGT.

8. Completion of reliefs will be reported by wire to Hdqs. YORK & LANCS.

9. O.C. Cos. will render a return by 10 am of number of "rifles" available for trenches.

10. Necessary reconnaissances will be carried out in the afternoon.

11. Guides will be @ the Barrier KEMMEL - LA CLYTTE ROAD @ 8.30pm. Coy Guides for H2, H3, H5 M.G. " H3, S.P. 12

12. Order of March M.G. Detachments
    H 2 Garrison
    H 3   "
    H 5   "
    Transport

Copies to:-

No 1 War Diary
" 2 1st York Lancs
" 3 Capt Deed
" 4   " Harris
" 5   " Fawcett
" 6   " Briggs

(sd) J. C. Milnes
Capt Adj.
5th Kingsown (R.L.R.)

Operation Orders No 4
by
Major E.C. Cadman
Cmdg. 5th Bn. The Kingstown (R.L.R.)

Copy No.1

15-8-15.

1. A & C Cos. will relieve 2 Cos. 6th Leicester Regt. attached to 2/Kingstown Regt. in H2, H3, H5 trenches, tonight.

2. Companies will parade @ 7pm & move off @ 7-30pm.
They will not pass the Barrier, KEMMEL LA CLYTTE RD. before 8-15 pm.

3. Three signallers will relieve signallers in H2 and 3 signallers in H5 trench. Two linesmen will be attached to H2 trench.
Signallers will relieve in trenches before 2pm. They will report relief complete by wire to Hdqrs. 2/Kingstown.

4. Two Stretcher Bearers will accompany each of the three garrisons. H2. H3. & H5.

5. C.S.Ms. will proceed to trenches @ 2pm to take over trench stores.

6. Water bottles to be filled, one day's rations & two sandbags per man will be carried.

7. Capt. Fawcett will be in charge of the party. Party will be attached to 2/Kingsdown

8. Completion of relief will be reported to HdQrs 2/Kingsdown.

9. Order of march.
   H 2 Garrison
   H 3   "
   H 5   "
   Transport.

10. As soon as relief is complete a nominal roll of sentries will be posted in each bay @ once

Copy No. 1 War Diary
     2 2/Kingsdown
     3 Capt. Fawcett
     4 "   Briggs.

(sd) J.C.Milnes
            Capt. Adj.
5th Kingsdown (R.L.R.)

Operation Orders No. 5
by
Major E. C. Cadman   Copy No. 1
Cmdg 5th Bn. The King's Own (R.L.R.)

Ref. Sheet 28   17-8-15

1. The Battalion will relieve the
Northumberland Fusiliers in the
following trenches tonight:-
    G 4   35 men
    G 4a   50   "
    New Sap   65   "   & 1 Machine Gun
    H. 1   55   "
    S.P. 11   50   "   & 1 Machine Gun

The garrison of H 2 & H 3 will remain
as at present.
The garrison of H 5 will be made up
by 25 men of this Bn. and the
remainder by 1 York. Lanc. Regt. This
garrison will come under command
of O.C. 1st York Lanc. Regt.

2. Machine Gun team in S.P. 12
will be relieved by 1st York Lancs.
The gun will be handed over to York
Lanc detachment.
5th King's Own detachment will
report to Lt Mansfield in S.P. 11

trench after relief

3. After Garrison in H5 (less 25 men) have been relieved by 1 York Lancs. they will proceed to relieve Garrison of H1 trench. Garrison of H1 will made up to 55 men from H2 & H3 trenches.
Capt Fawcett will supervise relief.

4. <u>Garrisons</u>

G4	35 men	} 85 B. Coy.	Capt. Deob
G4a	50 "		Lt. Parkinson
New Sap	65 men	} 95 D. Coy.	Capt. Harris
S.P. 11	30		Lt. Mansfield
H1	55 men	55 H5 Garrison	Lt. Sunnucks

5. On completion of relief Brigade front will be divided into three sectors.

  Right Sector 5" Kings Own
  Centre " 1st York Lancs
  Left " 1st K.O.Y.L.I

Right sector will consist of following trenches:- G4, G4a, New Sap, H1, H2, H3, & S.P. 11.

Right sector headquarters will be @ Stables KEMMEL CHATEAU.

6. Six signallers & four wiremen will report @ 2 p.m. @ Hdqrs. Northumberland Fusiliers to take over telephones in their trenches.

7. CSM of B. Coy will take over trenches in G.4 & G.4a
   CSM of D. Coy.   do.   New Sap & S.P. 11
   CSM of A. Coy.   do.   H.1

8. Completion of relief will be reported to Hdqrs. Right Section Stables, KEMMEL CHATEAU.

9. List of trench stores taken over from North. Fusiliers will be sent to Hdqrs. as soon as possible after reliefs are completed.

10. Each man will carry 3 sandbags & water bottles will be filled. One day's rations will be carried by the men.

11. <u>Order of March.</u>   <u>Guides</u>
        Hdqrs   NIL
        M.G. Detachment   1 guide from N.F.
        New Sap Garrison   for Sap.
        G.4   1 guide from N.F.
        G.4a   "
        S.P. 11
    Guides will be at barrier N.20.b"6.8
                                    at 8 p.m.

12. Nominal Rolls of Sentries will be posted in all bays in all trenches and M.G. positions as soon as reliefs are completed.

13. Reports will be sent in as follows:

    for A. Coy.   Capt. Fawcett
        B "   "   Deed
        C "   "   Brigg
        D "   "   Harriss
    (less S.P. 11 garrison)

S.P. 11 garrison
M.Gs.   Lt. Mansfield

After completion of reliefs O.C.'s A.B.C.D. Cos. will send two orderlies per company back to HdQrs.

Copies issued to:
1. War Diary
2. York Lants
3. 2 Kingsown
4. North Fusilier
5. Capt. Fawcett
6. " Deed
7. " Brigg
8. " Harriss
9. Q.master
10. M.G. Officer

(sd) J.C. Milnes
Capt. A/c
5th Kingsown (R.L.R.)

Copy No 1

Operation Order No 6. by Major E C Cadman commanding 1/5th Bn The King's Own R. Lanc Regt.

1. On night of 22-23rd inst

  (a) 3rd Monmouth Regt will relieve 5 King's Own in the Right Sector and their 25 men in H 5.

  (b) The ~~two~~ machine guns in New Sap & H3 will not be withdrawn but the team of the 5 King's Own in New Sap will be relieved by a team of 1/ KOYLI. and the team in H 3 will be relieved by a team of 2/ King's Own.
The machine gun and team in S.P. 11 will be relieved by the machine gun and team of 3 Monmouth Regt.

  (c) ~~Guides~~ Lt Mansfield will send one guide from each of the 3 machine gun emplacements to be at Hdqrs RIGHT SECTOR at 7-0 pm.
One guide per trench
One guide per machine gun } will meet 3 Monmouth
One guide for transport } Regt at cross roads
One guide for Hdqrs. } N. 20.k. q. 6. at 7.45 pm
Each guide will carry a chit showing which party he is to guide.

  (d) 3 Monmouth Signallers will take over at 3-0 pm

  (e) Major E.C. Cadman 5/ King's Own will command until relief is complete.

  (f) Relief will be reported by wire to Hdqrs RIGHT SECTOR as follows.

    G4 and G4a by Capt DEED.
    New Sap   — — HARRISS.
    H1, H2 and H3 — — FAWCETT.
    S.P. 11 and 3 M.G — Lt MANSFIELD.

2. On relief parties will march back independently to bivouacs last occupied by Battalion.

3. (a) M.G. limber for gun in S.P. 11 will be at DUMP at 9-0 pm.

  (b) Officers chargers will be at Hdqrs RIGHT SECTOR at 10-0 pm.

1. (a). G4a – Trench boards lifted, cleaned & replaced in one traverse.

   New Sap – 5ft of parapet rebuilt – Minor repairs to parapet

   H2   20 yds parapet retopped.
         10   "   parados
         One new traverse built
         300 Sandbags filled.

   H3   2 new banquettes built.
         8 yds of parapet thickened and retopped
         100 sandbags filled.

   (b) G4 – Trench scraped and trench boards laid in 2 traverses
       H1   4 yds parapet rebuilt.
             1 traverse rebuilt.
             2½ yds parados rebuilt.

   (c) C.T. right of G4a to G4 – Trench cleaned and 6 trench boards laid
       C.T. H1 to New Sap – Improvement continued.
       C.T. H1 to H5 – Draining & boarding floor

   (d) G4   Stakes driven in and barbed wire fixed for 12 yds along front
       H1   Wire repaired

3. New slip trenches in H1 and New Sap are being deepened and lengthened.

Op Ors cont'd

4. All Water tins will be ~~sent down to DUMP by 9.15 pm.~~ carried down when garrisons are relieved and handed over to Transport at the DUMP.

5. Periscopes will be handed over to 3/ Monmouth Regt.

6. List of Trench Stores handed over will be sent to Hdqrs as soon as possible.

Relief of H5.

Operation Orders No. 7
by
Major E. C. Cadman   Copy No. 1
Cmdg. 5th The King's Own (R.L.R.)

28-8-15

Ref. Sheet 28

1. The Battalion will relieve the 3rd Monmouth. Regt. in the following trenches tonight.
   G.4
   G.4a
   New Sap.   1 Machine Gun
   H.1
   S.P.11   1 Machine Gun
   H.2
   H.3   1 Machine Gun

2. Machine Gun teams will relieve M.G. teams in New Sap, S.P.11 and H.3.

3. Ten signallers and four wiremen will report @ Hdqrs Right Sector @ 7 pm. to take over ~~trenches~~ telephones in trenches.

4. C.S.M. of B Coy. will take over trenches in G.4 & G.4a

C.S.M. of D Coy. — New Sap - S.P. 11

C.S.M. of H Coy. }
do   C   "   }   H 1 - 2 - 3

5. Completion of relief will be
reported to Hdqrs Right Sector.

6. List of trench stores taken over
will be sent to Hdqrs as soon
as possible after relief is complete.

7. C-S-M. will report at Hd-Qrs. Right Sector
at 4-0 p.m. for taking over trenches.

8. S-M. Byrne will report at H.Qrs Right
Sector to take over Batt'n Head Qrs.

9. Two Stretcher Bearers per Coy. will proceed
to trenches with their respective companies

10. Each man will carry 3 Sandbags. Water
bottles to be filled. One day's rations
will be carried on the man.

11. Ten petrol cans of water per Coy. will
be taken to the dump. These will be
picked up by Coys. when passing dump
and taken up to trenches.

12. Nominal rolls of sentries will be posted in all bays in all trenches, as soon as relief is complete.

13. Reports will be sent in as follows:-
    A Coy   Capt Fawcett
    B "   Lieut Sunnucks
    C "   Capt. Briggs
    D less }   Capt Harriss
    S.P. 11 Garrison }
    S.P. 11 garrison & } Lieut Mansfield
    M. Guns.   }

14. After completion of relief Coys. A B C & D will send two orderlies per Coy. back to Head Quarters.

15. Battalion will parade at 5-45 pm and move off at 6-0 pm. in the following order

    M.G. detachments.
    NEW SAP Garrison.
    G 4
    G 4a
    H 1, 2 & 3.
    S.P. 11
    HEAD QUARTERS.
    TRANSPORT

16. Guides will be at the barrier N20b 6.8 at 7-15 pm.

17. Garrisons

B. { G 4   Lt Sunnucks & Lt Boys-Stones 3 6 ~~rifles~~ Other Ranks
    { G 4a ~~Gardiner~~ Ott Lt Cattell   5 0   "   "

D { NEW SAP. { Capt Harriss Lt Knox   6 4   "   "
  {   { Lt Bedford
  { S.P. 11   Lt Mansfield & Lt Harrold   3 2

A & C { H 1 Lt Parkinson ~~~~ Lt Monks   ~~~~ 4 0
      { H 2 Capt Fawcett ~~~~ ~~Lt~~   ~~6 0~~ 4 0
      { H 3 Capt Briggs Lt Lloyd Gardiner ~~5~~ 4 0
      { H 5   × 5

Hd-Qrs. { Lt Hyatt Phipp.

18. Surplus men over and above garrisons will form Head Quarter Coy under Lieut Hyatt Phipp.

19. Garrisons will be ~~exclusive~~ of Machine gunners, Signallers, Bomben & Stretcher Bearers.

20. One officer per Company will proceed to the trenches with the C.S.M. Officers to be detailed by their C.O.

Copies issued to:—
1 War Diary
2 3 Monmouths
3 Capt Fawcett
4 Lt Sunnicks
5 Capt Briggs
6 " Harriss
7 Lt 2m Hodgkinson
8 M.G. Officer

5th Bn The Kings Own
(R.L.R.)

Operation Orders No. 7
by
Major E. C. Cadman   Copy No. 9
Cmdg. 5th Bn. The King's Own (R.L.R.)

28-8-15

Ref. Sheet 78

1. The Battalion will relieve the
3rd Monmouth Regt. in the following
trenches tonight
  G 4
  G 4 a
  New Sap.   1 Machine Gun
  S P 11   1 do.
  H 1
  H 2
  H 3   do.

2. Machine Gun Teams will relieve M.G.
Teams in New Sap. S P 11 & H 3

3. Ten signallers & four wiremen will
report @ Hdqrs. Right Sector @ 2 p.m.
to take over telephones in trenches

4. O.S.M. of B Co. will take over trenches
  D } G 4 & G 4 a
  A } New Sap & S P 11
  C   H 1. 2. 3.

5. Completion of relief will be reported to Hdqrs. Right Sector

6. List of trench stores taken over will be sent to Hdqrs as soon as possible after relief is complete

7. C.S.M. will report @ Hdqrs. R.S. @ 4 p.m. for taking over trenches

8. S.M. Byrne will report @ Hdqrs R.S. to take over Bn. Hdqrs.

9. Two S.Bs per Coy. will proceed to trenches with their respective Coys.

10. Each man will carry 3 sandbags water bottles filled & one day's rations

11. Ten patrols cans of water per coy. will be taken to the dump. These will be picked up by Coy. when passing dump & taken up to trenches

12. Nominal rolls of sentries will be posted in all bays in all trenches as soon as relief is complete

13. Reports will be sent as as follows:
A Coy. Capt Egward
B   Lt Immacks

```
        C Coy         }   Capt Briggs
        D less        }   Harriss
S.P.11 Garrison       }
S.P.11 Garrison       }
        M Guns        }   Lt. Mansfield
```

14. After completion of relief OC ABCD will send two orderlies back to Hdqrs.

15. Bn will parade @ 5-45 pm & move off @ 6 pm @ 5 minute intervals, in following order.

    M.G. detachments
    New Sap Garrison
    G 4
    G 4a
    H 1. 2. 3
    S.P. 11
    Head Quarters
    Transport

16. Guides will be @ Barrier N30668 @ 7-15 pm.

17. Garrisons

B.   G 4 & McGunners Boys Stones   35 orank.
B.   G 4a   Ogle & Carrell   50

D. { New Cap. Capt Harris   65 o ranks
        Lt. Knox Bedford
   { SP 11 Lt. Mansfield Harrold 30 "

A&C { H 1 Lt Parkinson Lt. Monks   45 "
     { H 2 Capt Fawcus Lt Gardiner 60 "
     { H 3   Briggs Lt Lloyd   45 "

Hdqrs. Lt. Shipp

18 Surplus men over & above
    garrisons will form Hdqr. Coy. under
    Lt. Shipp.

19 Garrisons will be inclusive
    of M. Gunners, Signallers, Linesmen
    & S. Bearers

20 One officer per Coy. will proceed
    to the trenches with the CSM.
    Officers to be detailed by O.C. Cos

                    Lt (SS) H Bell Lt & adj.
                    5th Bn. The Kingsown
                              (R.L.R.)

Operation Order no 13 Copy 1
by
Lt Col Cadman Cmdg. 5th Kingsdown (R.L.R.)

1. On 23rd Sept. the 83rd Bde. will march to billets about OUTTERSTEENE via LOCRE, BAILLEUL — OUTTERSTEENE Road.

2. Starting point LOCRE CHURCH.
   Order of march of Brigade.
   Billeting parties of all units as a formed body under   } 8 a.m.
        Capt. BRAZIER 1st K.O.Y.L.I.
   Brigade H.Qrs.
   1st York. Lanc. Regt.
   2nd Kings Own Regt.
   2nd East Yorks Regt.
   1st K.O.Y.L.I. Regt.
   5th Kings Own Regt.   9-40 a.m.
   2 Ambulances 84th F.A.   9-50 a.m.

   Clearing up parties of all units
   as a formed body under   } 11 a.m.
   Capt. CAREW. R. Dublin Fusiliers

3. (a) 2 Lt. Lloyd, 2nd Lt Bell, one L/C. from each Coy. & 7 men from A. Coy. are detailed as a rearguard to march in rear of the Ambulances & collect any stragglers falling behind the Brigade.

(b) 1 monks & 1 N.C.O. per Coy. will march in rear of the perkine Transport to collect stragglers from this Bn.

(c) No individuals or small parties will be allowed to march except as laid down in para. 2 of this O.O.

(d) Attention is drawn to Bde. Bde. Standing Orders for marches reissued herewith. These orders will be strictly adhered to.

(e) There must be no check when marching into billets. Billeting parties will meet Cos. well back on the line of march & conduct Cos. transport vehicles direct to their appointed places, leaving the road clear for troops following them.

4. The Corps Commander will be in Bailleul to watch the Bde. pass through. Compliments will be paid to all General officers.

5. Brigade HdQrs. will be at OUTTERSTEENE on conclusion of the march.

6. Parade 8 a.m.
Order of march of Battalion
Headquarters
A Coy
B "
C "
D "

M.G. Section
↗ S. Bearers
M. Gun Limber

Tool limbers
S.A.A. Carts
Water Carts
Travelling Kitchens
Officers Mess Cart
Spare Horses (led)
Men marching with 1st line Transport under R.S.M. Byrne.
M.O. & rear party.

Transport will join the Bn. at Hyde Park Corner.

Pack horses will march with the Cos. & M.G. limbers.

7. Billeting Party.

The following are detailed as billeting party.

Lt. L.M. Hodgkinson
P.S. Benson
Hesketh   Cyclist
Barrow
Hartley   B. Stoneman
Heridge   D. "
Brocklank   Groom.

8 Clearing up party is detailed as follows:
2 Lt. Boys Stones
Cpl. Preston
8 men from C. Coy

9. Officers kits will be loaded @ 7-30 am.
   Mess   do
   2/M Stores   do
   O.Room Boxes   do
   Cookers will be ready to leave @ 7-30 am

10. During halts the heads of all riding, pack & spare horses will be turned to the centre of the road.

11. All fittings, boxes in officers huts, poles & sheets etc must be removed & ~~huts~~ trenches, if any, filled in by 7 am.

12. On arrival in new billets the following orders will be strictly enforced. Any man contravening same will be immediately arrested.
    "No smoking, lights or striking of matches will be allowed in any barn without a written order from the Adjutant"

13. Breakfast 6-30 am.
    All cooking utensils must be returned to cookhouse in clean condition by 7 am.

14. Every man, including Transport M/s, T.Bs. & all men regimentally employed will carry his complete equipment.

(Sd) J.C. Milnes
Capt Adj

5th Bn. THE KING'S OWN (R. LANC. REGT.)

83rd Bde.
28th Div.

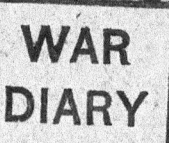

WAR DIARY

1/5th K. O. R. L.

SEPTEMBER

1 9 1 5

WAR DIARY or INTELLIGENCE SUMMARY

Army Form C. 2118.

(Erase heading not required.)

Instructions regarding War Diaries and Intelligence Summaries are contained in F.S. Regs., Part II. and the Staff Manual respectively. Title pages will be prepared in manuscript.

Hour, Date, Place	Summary of Events and Information	Remarks and references to Appendices
1-9-18 KEMMEL	Battalion in the trenches – RIGHT SECTOR Ianchone. C.T. from C.s to listening post continued. Sandbags & parados rebuilt. Dug outs built. Normal. Situation. Operations. Artillery was active & persistent from our side. Artillery communication. Artillery and support trenches as during the disturbance by enemy. Barrage the parapet as in case of attack by enemy. Maximum hours minimum hours 1. 10 a.m. 16.00 2. 5 a.m. 3. 4 p.m.	
2-9-18 KEMMEL	Work done. Normal. Situation. Enemy active. Enemy artillery gently examined German wire from a distance of 10 yds. Then moved up support & passed what able to men food & ammunition. 1. Wire good & strong condition 2. Sandbags by support post 3' 6" about 10' & unit & 30' units. Wine near trench disfavored.	

Army Form C. 2118.

WAR DIARY
or
INTELLIGENCE SUMMARY

(Erase heading not required.)

Instructions regarding War Diaries and Intelligence Summaries are contained in F. S. Regs, Part II. and the Staff Manual respectively. Title pages will be prepared in manuscript.

Hour, Date, Place	Summary of Events and Information	Remarks and references to Appendices
3-9-15 KEMMEL	General — No top cover, Mine close to parapet and front lire in front. No top wire no long grass.	
	Work done. General improvement to trenches	
	Situation. Normal	
	General. Equal artillery activity by both sides. 5 Battalion reliefs and trench known. Snipers from again formed into two sections. Three reserve platoons to billets as SCHERPENBERG. Relief completed by 7-15 p.m.	
4-9-15 SCHERPENBERG	Inspection of arms & equipment. 50 men as Carrying Party. 80 men as working party on Scherpenberg lines	
5. 9. 15. do.	Baths at HESTOUTRE General training.	
6. 9. 15. do.	Special instruction was given to bombing during general training. During afternoon the enemy shelled SCHERPENBERG district.	

1247 W 3299 200,000 (E) 8/14 J.B.C. & A. Forms/C. 2118/11.

Army Form C. 2118.

WAR DIARY
or
INTELLIGENCE SUMMARY

(Erase heading not required.)

Instructions regarding War Diaries and Intelligence Summaries are contained in F. S. Regs., Part II. and the Staff Manual respectively. Title pages will be prepared in manuscript.

Hour, Date, Place	Summary of Events and Information	Remarks and references to Appendices
7.9.15 SCHERPENBERG	Draft of 30 other ranks received from 3/5 Bn. General training resumed.	
8.9.15 do.	A + C Companies are relieved by B + D Cos. Some under command of 2nd the platoon. The following trenches manned:— G + a 40 C + 35 H 1 a 50 M.G. } Regtl Section H 1 33 S.P. 11 25 M.G.	
9.9.15 do. 2pm	Inspection of arms & equipment Machine gun practices on the range.	
10.9.15 do.	The following trenches were furnished 8 Officers 153 other ranks Enemy aeroplanes very active.	
11.9.15 do.	General movement. Special arrangements to handle bayonet fighting 130 men furnished for working carrying parties. Divine Service for all denominations	
12.9.15 do.	Inspection of arms & equipment	

WAR DIARY or INTELLIGENCE SUMMARY

Army Form C. 2118.

(Erase heading not required.)

Hour, Date, Place	Summary of Events and Information	Remarks and references to Appendices
13-9-15 SCHERPENBERG	General training	
14-9-15 do.	115 men detailed for fatigues. General training. Adjt. visited by McAngus Staff	
15-9-15 do.	A. Cosgrove relieved by B.T.O. to rifle decon (detachment from teams) training done by Companies in Company lines.	
16-9-15 do.	Baths at WESTOUTRE. Inspection of arms & equipment. Working Party and Fatigues provided as night - 170 men	
17-9-15 do.	General training 60 men for carrying parties	
18-9-15 do.	General training. Enemy aeroplane active, also our own. No rifles. Bombs & flares dropped down near LA CLYTTE.	
19-9-15 do.	Divine Services for all denominations	

WAR DIARY
or
INTELLIGENCE SUMMARY

(Erase heading not required.)

Army Form C. 2118.

Instructions regarding War Diaries and Intelligence Summaries are contained in F. S. Regs., Part II. and the Staff Manual respectively. Title pages will be prepared in manuscript.

Hour, Date, Place	Summary of Events and Information	Remarks and references to Appendices
20.9.15 SCHERPENBERG	General training.	
21.9.15 do.	Coy relieved by 2nd Canadians. Transport inspected by Brigadier for Revn show.	
22.9.15 do.	R Coy at WESTOUTRE bath. A Coy on Route march (2 hours.)	
23.9.15 do.	Battalion on Route march. General training	
24.9.15 OUTTERSTEENE	Brigade relieved by Canadians. Moved to billets at OUTTERSTEENE. Bn was complimented by Sir Chas Fergusson on marching through BAILLEUL and arrived in its billets about noon. Preparations made for sudden move ordered by G.O.C. in Command.	
25.9.15 do	Dances to be ready to move at 2 hours notice at 6 p.m.	
26.9.15 do.	Orders to move received at 3. a.m. Bn. moves off by route of march at 8 am toward ROBECQ where halt was made for dinner. March continued during afternoon toward BETHUNE but eventually Bn. returned to billets near ROBECQ	

Army Form C. 2118.

WAR DIARY
or
INTELLIGENCE SUMMARY
(Erase heading not required.)

Hour, Date, Place	Summary of Events and Information	Remarks and references to Appendices
27-9-15 ROBECQ	Bn. moved at noon to FOYELLES by lorries. Where night was spent in open in fields without any cover.	
28-9-15 do	Bn. marched bivouac round villages during afternoon in case enemy artillery responded our heavy bombardment. 200 new recruits @ night for fatigue.	
29-9-15 do	Bn standing to from 10-30 a.m. to 6-15 p.m. when they moved into reserve trenches at VERMELLES	
30-9-15 do	Bn still in reserve trenches	

E. Willoughby
2ic 2m
for O.C. 5"Bn The Kings own (R.L.R.)

83rd Bde.
28th Div.

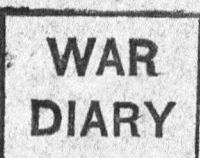

21.10.15.
Battalion transferred to 2nd Bde. 1st Div.

1/5th K. O. R. L.

OCTOBER

1 9 1 5

Confidential.

October 1915.

WAR DIARY
or
INTELLIGENCE SUMMARY

Army Form C. 2118.

5th BN. THE KING'S OWN (R. LANC. REGT.)

(Erase heading not required.)

Instructions regarding War Diaries and Intelligence Summaries are contained in F. S. Regs., Part II. and the Staff Manual respectively. Title pages will be prepared in manuscript.

Hour, Date, Place	Summary of Events and Information	Remarks and references to Appendices
Oct 1st. VERMELLES	Battalion in reserve trenches at VERMELLES. "Standing to" at different parts of day - enemy counter-attacks. Battalion relieved at night by 5th King's Shropshire Regt. Arrived in billets at ANNEQUIN at 3-0 a.m.	
Oct. 2nd. ANNEQUIN.	In billets. Cleaning up and resting. Sudden orders to proceed to trenches S.E. of VERMELLES to support the 84th Brigade. 350 men detailed by Brigade Major 84th Brigade for fatigue, bombs, ammunition, water and ration carrying.	
Oct. 3rd. VERMELLES [HULLUCH TRENCHES]	Whole battalion arrived in 2nd and support trenches at 4 a.m. Great activity on part of our artillery. Bombing sorties by own and enemy bombers. At night 83rd Brigade occupy trenches held by 64th Brigade. Battalion moves to reserve trenches occupied on Oct 1st.	
Oct 4th HULLUCH TRENCHES	In reserve trenches. Supporting 83rd Brigade.	
Oct 5th do	Reserve trenches as on 4th. Brigade relieved by Guards Brigade at night Battn. proceeds to billets at ANNEQUIN. Arrived 5-30 a.m. 6th Oct.	

Confidential.

Army Form C. 2118.

2.

WAR DIARY
or
INTELLIGENCE SUMMARY

(Erase heading not required.)

5th BN. THE KING'S OWN (R. LANC. REGT.)

Hour, Date, Place	Summary of Events and Information	Remarks and references to Appendices
Oct. 6th ANNEQUIN.	In billets at ANNEQUIN. Cleaning of arms and equipment. Orders received to move. Battalion moved to farm. Billets through BETHUNE to GONNEHEM [Pencil below]. Arrived at 7-0 pm. Battn. Headquarters CENSE au VALLEE.	
Oct. 7th GONNEHEM. [CENSE a VALLEE]	Resting. Cleaning of arms and equipment	
Oct. 8th do.	General training. Company Close Order drill. Bombing Practice in trenches near GONNEHEM.	
Oct. 9th do.	Training. Special instruction and practice in bombing	
Oct. 10th do.	Divine Service for all denominations in morning. Company drill in afternoon.	
Oct. 11th do.	Baths at GONNEHEM, 7 a.m - 5 p.m. General training a. Trench warfare, bombing trenches &c. b. Company drill.	

Confidential

WAR DIARY
or
INTELLIGENCE SUMMARY
(Erase heading not required.)

Army Form C. 2118.

5th BN. THE KINGS OWN (R. LANC. REGT.)

Instructions regarding War Diaries and Intelligence Summaries are contained in F. S. Regs., Part II. and the Staff Manual respectively. Title pages will be prepared in manuscript.

Hour, Date, Place	Summary of Events and Information	Remarks and references to Appendices
Oct. 12th GONNEHEM [CENSE à VALLÉE]	Training a. Company order drill b. Bombing practice	
Oct. 13th do.	83rd Brigade inspected by G.O.C. 28th Division on field near GONNEHEM. Battn. paraded at 8.0 a.m. & march to field for inspection parade. Bombing practice in afternoon.	
Oct. 14th do.	Trench warfare and bombing trench practice. Night digging - from 6-7 p.m.	
Oct. 15th {do. {FERME du ROI}	Physical training. Bombing practice. Battn. moves at 4-29 p.m. in accordance with 83rd Brigade Op. Order no. 78. by Brig-Gen. H.S.L. Ravenshaw. Arrived in billets at 9-30 p.m. [FERME du ROI]. BETHUNE.	Attached.
Oct. 16th FERME du ROI [BETHUNE]	Battalion parade at 3-0 p.m. Ordered to move.	
Oct. 17th FERME du ROI.	Battalion moves off at 10-15 a.m. As 83rd Brigade Op. Orders no. 79. by Brig-Gen. H.S.L. Ravenshaw.	Attached.

Confidential.

4.

Army Form C. 2118.

WAR DIARY
or
INTELLIGENCE SUMMARY
(Erase heading not required.)

5th BN. THE KINGS OWN (R. LANC. REGT.)

Instructions regarding War Diaries and Intelligence Summaries are contained in F. S. Regs., Part II. and the Staff Manual respectively. Title pages will be prepared in manuscript.

Hour, Date, Place	Summary of Events and Information	Remarks and references to Appendices
Oct. 17th. LE PREOL.	Officers reconnoitre trenches at CUINCHY.	
Oct. 18th. do.	Trenches further reconnoitred by officers (CUINCHY). Four machine-gun teams with guns proceed to trenches to with 2nd Kings Own 1 " K.O.Y.L.I.	
Oct. 19th. do.	Training. Working party of 1 officer 50 O.R found in morning. " " 6 " 300 " evening 1 officer 2/1st Northumbrian Fuses to R.E. Returned at midnight.	
Oct. 20th. do.	General training in the afternoon. 6 men ; time expired sent to Base for passage to England. 5 " returned to unit from hare hospital. Of-Order 80 reinforcements from 63rd Brigade.	
Oct. 21st. GONNEHEM. { L'ECLEME – ROBECQ	Battalion moves to billets previously occupied at GONNEHEM. Arrived 2-30 p.m. Received further orders to move to billets on L'ECLEME – ROBECQ Road. Arrived at 8-0 p.m. Battalion is transferred to IVth Corps 1st Division 2nd Brigade.	

Confidential

Army Form C. 2118.

WAR DIARY
or
INTELLIGENCE SUMMARY
(Erase heading not required.)

5th BN. THE KINGS OWN (R. LANC. REGT.)

Instructions regarding War Diaries and Intelligence Summaries are contained in F.S. Regs., Part II. and the Staff Manual respectively. Title pages will be prepared in manuscript.

Hour, Date, Place	Summary of Events and Information	Remarks and references to Appendices
Oct 21st. L'ECLEME - ROBECQ.	Five officers as detailed transferred to 2nd Bn. Kings Own (Reserve Regt.) 2/Lieuts. D.H.KNOX; G.M.LLOYD; C.E.MONKS; W.HARROLD; and H.A.BEDFORD. [10th K.O.R.L.R] [10th K.O.R.L.R] [10th N.STAFFS] [10th N.STAFFS] [10th K.O.R.L.R].	Attached 5th Kings Own.
	2/Lieut. D.B.GOWER (10th K.O.R.L.R) attached 5th Kings Own. Transferred to ROYAL NAVAL RESERVE.	
	Four officers: 2/Lt LLOYD EVANS, 2/Lt. HINTON, " GILCHRIST, " CATTELL } Detailed for entraining duties at BETHUNE. (28 Divn)	
	One officer LT. SUNNUCKS } Entraining duties at LILLERS. 41 other ranks	
Oct 22nd. L'ECLEME - ROBECQ.	Battn. moves to 2nd Brigade area at ECQUEDECQUES via L'ECLEME and LILLERS.	
ECQUEDECQUES.	Arrived in new billets at 1-0 p.m.	
Oct 23rd. ECQUEDECQUES.	Battalion training per 2nd Brigade training programme.	

Army Form C. 2118.

WAR DIARY
or
INTELLIGENCE SUMMARY

5th BN. THE KING'S OWN (R. LANC. REGT.)

(Erase heading not required.)

Hour, Date, Place	Summary of Events and Information	Remarks and references to Appendices
Oct. 24th. ECQUEDECQUES	Church services for C of E and R.C. catholics. 28 men, 3 N.C.O's detailed for 2nd Brigade Grenade school at LILLERS. 1 N.C.O, 8 men detailed for wiring course at LILLERS by Brigade arrangements. Officers & men detailed for entraining 26th Div. rejoin battalion.	
Oct. 25th do.	General training.	
Oct. 26th do.	Battalion training. Courses held for N.C.O's in Musketry, Physical training, Bayonet fighting } under officers and Regt. S. Major.	
Oct. 27th do.	Battalion inspected by G.O.C. 2nd Brigade Brig-Gen THUILLIER (Tempy commanding Division) at LILLERS. 10-30 a.m. Parade 9 a.m. in full marching order.	
Oct. 28th do.	Composite battalion of 2nd Brigade units inspected by His Majesty the King. 5th King's Own supply 5 officers and 200 men. Rest of Battalion, Route march from 8-30 a.m - 1 p.m. Wet day.	

WAR DIARY or INTELLIGENCE SUMMARY

(Erase heading not required.)

Army Form C. 2118.

5th BN. THE KING'S OWN (R. LANC. REGT.)

Hour, Date, Place	Summary of Events and Information	Remarks and references to Appendices
Oct. 29th ECQUEDÉCQUES	No morning parades. General training in afternoon. Lecture on "FROSTBITE" at Theatre LILLERS by Major Hogarth 2nd Field Ambulance.	
Oct. 30th do.	Bombing practice and training. Lecture to officers and junior N.C.O.'s on ENTRENCHING by Capt. Fawcett	
Oct. 31st do.	Divine Service for all denominations.	

J. Lawes
Lieut-Col.
Commanding 5th BN. THE KING'S OWN (R. LANC. REGT.)
31/X/15.

SECRET.   Copy No. 6

Operation Order No. 78.

by

Brigadier General R.R.L.Ravenshaw C.M.G.
Commanding 83rd Infantry Brigade.

Reference, BETHUNE (Combined sheet)   15th October 1915.
           /40,000.

1. The Brigade will march to Billetting area at 4 p.m.

2. Order of march:-

                    Brigade Headquarters   4 p.m.
                    8/King's Own Regt.   4.3 p.m.
                    1/K.O.Y.L.I.   4.12 p.m.
                    1/York & Lancaster R.   4.20 p.m.
                    5/King's Own Regt.   4.29 p.m.
                    ~~24th Field Ambulance~~ ~~4.37 p.m.~~ /M

Starting point Forked roads K.22.b.9.9.

6/East Yorkshire Regt. will march independently via OBLINGHEM -
BETHUNE to billets in ESSARS. Starting at 4.40 p.m.

3. The Brigade will be billetted as follows:-

                    8/King's Own Regt   LE PREOL
                    1/K.O.Y.L.I.   LE QUESNOY
                    1/York & Lancaster R.   BEUVRY
                    5/King's Own Regt.   FERME de ROI
                    6/East Yorkshire Regt.   ESSARS
                    ~~24th Field Ambulance~~ BEUVRY /M

4. Guides from 7th Division will meet units at Forked roads
   K.22.b.9.9. to guide them to their billets. Guide will meet
   6/King's Own at Forked roads E.11.b.5.9.

5. Brigade Headquarters will be at BEUVRY.
                                              E.11.b.5.9.
Issued at   p.m.

Copy no. 1 War Diary
        2   8/King's Own
        3   6/East Yorks
        4   1/K.O.Y.L.I.   Major,
        5   1/York & Lancs
        6   5/King's Own   Brigade Major,
        7   24th Field Ambulance.   83rd Infantry Brigade.

LE QUESNOY

SECRET.   OPERATION ORDERS NO, 79   Copy No....6.

                                         by

                    Brigadier General H.S.L.Ravenshaw, C.M.G.

                         Commanding 83rd Infantry Brigade,

Reference BETHUNE Combined Sheet, 1/40,000.   16th October, 1915.

1.   The 83rd Brigade will relieve the 22nd Brigade tomorrow.

2.   1/K.O.Y.L.I. will relieve the 2/Queens and take over from
        THE LANE to HANOVER STREET exclusive.

        2/King's Own will relieve the Welsh Fusiliers and take over
        from HANOVER STREET inclusive to CANAL.

        1st York & Lancaster will relieve the 2/Warwicks and be in
        Reserve in HARLEY STREET.

        2/East Yorks will move to LE PREOL, taking over billets
        from S.Staffords,

        5/King's Own will move to LE PREOL, taking over billets
        now occupied by the 2/King's Own.

3.   Units will march at the following times :- (by platoons.)
        1/K.O.Y.L.I. 9.30 a.m. guides at HARLEY STREET 11 a.m.
        2/King's Own 10.30 "   "   "   "   11.30 a.m.   By
        1/York & L. 11.30 "   "   "   "   12.15 p.m.   Platoons
        2/East Yorks 10 a.m. take over billets at   11 a.m.
        5/King's Own 10.30 a.m. "   "   "   "   11. 30 a.m.

4.   1/ K.O.Y.L.I. will find the Carrison for STAFFORD REDOUBT.

5.   1/York & Lancaster Regt. will place Machine Guns
                Two in PONT FIXE
                One in THE BULGE
                One on Canal Bank, to sweep the front of the
                Brigade on the left.

6.   The 34th Brigade R.F.A. will be covering the front of the
        Section.

7.   1st Line Transport of Bde. Hdqrs., 2/King's Own, 1/K.O.Y.L.I.
        and 1 /Y.& Lancaster Regts. will be parked about F.23 b.
        Brigade Transport Officer will select ground.
        1st Line Transport 2/E.Yorks. & 5/ King's Own will remain
        with Battalions at LE PREOL.

8.   Brigade Headquarters will move at 11 a.m. to CAMBRIN, A.19.d.6.3

Issued at 3 p.m.

Copy No.1   War Diary
        2   2/East Yorks
        3   2/King's Own
        4   1/K.O.Y.L.I.   Major.
        5   1/York & Lancaster R.
        6   5/King's Own   Brigade Major
        7   28th Division   83rd Infantry Brigade.
        8   22nd Brigade
        9   No.2 Coy.A.S.C.
       10   84th Field Ambulance
       11   C.O.Signals 83rd Bde
       12   M.G.Officer 83rd Bde

SECRET.   Copy No... 6

83rd BRIGADE OPERATION ORDER No.80.

Reference BETHUNE Combined Sheet   October 20th 1915.
          1/40,000.

1. The 83rd Infantry Brigade will be relieved by the 6th Inf. Brigade on October 21st.

2. The reliefs will be carried out in accordance with the accompanying table.

3. All trench stores and bombs will be handed over to the 6th Infantry Brigade and all Programme of work proposed and in hand.

4. The relief of the machine guns will be carried out in accordance with attached table. Arrangements will be made by Battalion Machine Gun Officers. Guides to be at HARLEY STREET at 8.30 a.m.

5. The 62nd Trench Mortar Battery will remain with the 6th Brigade.

6. The 2/1 Field Coy. R.E. will be relieved by the 11th Field Coy. R.E. and will move to the 83rd Infantry Brigade Area.

7. On relief units will march independantly to their destinations which will be detailed later. Movements by companies.

8. Completion of relief and arrival of battalions at their destination will be reported to Brigade Headquarters.

9. The G.O.C. 83rd Brigade will remain in Command until relief is completed.

10. All transport will be prepared to move to new area tomorrow morning. Orders will be issued later.

Issued at 1.15 p.m.

Copy No. 1 War Diary
       2 2/King's Own
       3 2/East Yorks
       4 1/K.O.Y.L.I.
       5 1/York & Lancas
       6 5/King's Own
       7 6th Inf. Bde.
       8 28th Divn.
       9 No.2 Coy. A.S.C.
      10 2/1 Field Coy. R.E.
      11 84th Field Ambulance
      12 62nd Trench M. Batty.
      13 Staff Capt. 83rd Bde
      14 O.C. Signals 83rd Bde

                                                        Captain
                                                    for Brigade Major
                                                  83rd Infantry Brigade.

U N I T	L I N E	RELIEVED BY	GARRISON IN AREA	GUIDES TO BE IN HARLEY ST.
1/K.O.Y.L.I.	From THE LANE to RIDLEY WALK inclusive	5/King's Liverpool R.	PARK LANE Redoubt STAFFORD REDOUBT	10 a.m.
1/K.O.Y.L.I.	From RIDLEY WALK exclusive to HANOVER ST. exclusive	2/South Staffords R.	BRICKSTACKS KEEP	11 a.m.
2/King's Own R.	From HANOVER ST. inclusive to CANAL	2/South Staffords R.	LOVERS Redoubt CABBAGE PATCH Redoubt.	11 a.m.
1/York & Lanca'r R.	Support Area	1/King's Regt.	GUINCHY S.P. CAMBRIN S.P. PONT FIXE	12 Noon.
2 Platoons 1/York & Lancaster Regt.	BRADDELL POINT	5/King's Liverpool		10 a.m.

MACHINE GUNS WILL BE RELIEVED AS FOLLOWS.

POSITION	RELIEVED BY
Railway Embankment PORTLAND PLACE B BRICKSTACKS.	South Staffords
GUN STREET WATERLOO PLACE SEYMOUR STREET OXFORD STREET	5/ Liverpools
CABBAGE PATCH IKEY TRENCH LOVERS REDOUBT.	1/King's Regt.
CUINCHY Support Point Machine Gun House STAFFORD REDOUBT BRADDELL REDOUBT	1/Herts Regt.

SECRET.   Copy No. 6

AFTER OPERATION ORDER No.80 83rd Brigade.

Reference, BETHUNE combined sheet. 1/40,000   20th October 1915.

1. On relief tomorrow units will march by BEUVRY – BETHUNE – OBLINGHEM to the same billetting areas they occupied when the Brigade were at GONNEHEM. Except that the 2/East Yorkshire Regt. with 1st Line transport will march at 10 a.m. by LE QUESNOY – BETHUNE – & OBLINGHEM to billets in LENGLET V.22.a.
   5/King's Own Regt. will await further orders.

2. The 1st Line transport of the Brigade less cookers and less transport of 2/East Yorks & 5/King's Own will march under the Brigade Transport Officer to the billetting area of the Brigade, and proceed to same fields as before, leaving ANNEQUIN at 10.30 a.m.

3. 2/King's Own 1/K.O.Y.L.I. 1/York & Lancs will march to about F.13 West of BEUVRY by Companies and from there by Battalions independantly.

4. 2/1 Northumbrian Field Co.R.E. will march to billets in farm V.18.b.9.3. at 9 a.m.

5. 84th Field Ambulance will occupy same billets as before in GONNEHEM.

Issued at 5-45 P.M.

Copy No. 1 War Diary
        2 2/King's Own
        3 2/East Yorks
        4 1/K.O.Y.L.I.
        5 1/York & Lancs
        6 5/King's Own
        7 6th Brigade
        8 28th Divn.
        9 84th Field Ambulance
       10 2/1 Northumbrian Fd.Co.R.E.
       11 No.2.Coy.A.S.C.
       12 62nd Trench M. Batty
       13 O.C. Signals 83rd Bde
       14 Staff Capt. 83rd Bde.

                                          Captain,
                                    for Brigade Major,
                                  83rd Infantry Brigade.